12/25/05

FURMAN BISHER

FACE TO FACE

*For Wes — with good wishes for
a Merrie Christmas, and more*

BY
FURMAN BISHER

Furman Bisher

SPORTS PUBLISHING L.L.C.

www.SportsPublishingLLC.com

ISBN: 1-58261-815-1

Publishers: Peter L. Bannon and Joseph J. Bannon Sr.
Senior managing editor: Susan M. Moyer
Acquisitions editor: Dean Reinke
Developmental editor: Erin Linden-Levy
Art director: K. Jeffrey Higgerson
Dust jacket design: Joseph Brumleve
Project manager: Kathryn R. Holleman
Imaging: Heidi Norsen and Dustin Hubbart
Vice president of sales and marketing: Kevin King
Media and promotions managers: Jonathan Patterson (regional),
  Randy Fouts (national), Maurey Williamson (print)

Printed in the United States of America

Sports Publishing L.L.C.
804 North Neil Street
Champaign, IL 61820

Phone: 1-877-424-2665
Fax: 217-363-2073
www.SportsPublishingLLC.com

To the men of Rutgers and Princeton football, who played the first game; to Aristides, who won the first Kentucky Derby; to Horace Rawlins, who won the first U.S. Open; to Ray Harroun, who won the first Indianapolis 500; to Red Byron, first NASCAR champion; to Jay Berwanger, first Heisman Trophy winner; to Dr. Naismith, first man of basketball; to all those who helped pave the way; and first and foremost, to Lynda.

— CONTENTS —

— INTRODUCTION —

All books, I'm assured, have to open with something like this, call it what you will. Introduction. Foreword. Acknowledgment. Whatever. Call this a Whatever.

It's sort of embarrassing to ask somebody, friend or bare acquaintance, to do one of these. Bing Crosby did an introduction for me, dictated by radiophone from his boat off Cabo San Lucas. Fitting to say that it sang.

Another time, Lewis Grizzard did one, and that indeed represented a hard turn in the road of journalism. Lewis had once worked for me, but he quit because he couldn't stand meetings or me. Didn't have another job to go to, but say this for him: When he applied for another job, he called on me for one of his references.

Time marched on and he later became one of the funniest entertainers in America, as a columnist and a standup comedian, and people still wonder if there isn't some way we can recycle him. We became friends again under a new set of ground rules, and began to see each other in an entirely different light. He had a writing style, which we'd never realized before. He was in demand on television. He was on Johnny Carson's show, several times. He became famous. He also became rich but had no sense about how to handle it all. Money didn't mean that much to him, once he accumulated a good supply.

Then came the time to ask him to do the introduction, to a book modestly titled *The Furman Bisher Collection*. Now, that was a turnaround.

What I'd anticipated was something in his tongue-in-cheek, biting column style. Good fun. Tweak the old boy a little bit. Instead, it was such a tribute I almost cried, and it still makes my blood run warm when I think of it. We had rekindled our friendship, but I had no idea what had been going through Lewis's head all those years.

Lewis Grizzard (left) and Furman Bisher. *Rich Mahan/AJC Staff*

I'm not going to reprint it here, much as I'd like to, but I will drop in a heart-tingler or two. Such as: "The words from other writers marched drone-like. Furman's dance."

Lewis wrote that? My God, I blushed.

I continue: "Young people ask me, 'How do I learn to be a writer?'

"I write them, 'Find somebody whose writing you admire, steal his or her style, and use it until you can come up with one of your own. That's how I began. I attempted to write just like Furman Bisher, and when I realized I couldn't, I wandered over someplace else.'"

Lucky for him. His wandering carried him off into the wild blue, into a level never approached by me. He far overshot his goal. He became rich and famous, I repeat, and was pillaged, never quite able to sort out who was a real friend and who was a hanger-on. So sad that such a talent should have been snuffed out at the age of 47. I never did get to write an introduction for one of Lewis's books—he even dedicated one to me—but he left me with something to remember him by, all in good humor: A large, black-headlined front page with the words:

"It's Not God-Damned Magazine, It's a NewsPaper!"

Ye gods, this has become more self-serving than introductory, and I apologize. Just call it the introduction I never got to write for Lewis. Other than this, you won't find him in this collection. I never interviewed him—for publication.

— JACK McKEON —

Senior Skipper

J ack McKeon is not your common garden-variety shrinking violet. He is mentally equipped to speak on most any subject on a moment's notice—especially baseball, and how a team should be managed. He should know. In 2003 he was managing his 16th team, 48 years and many leagues above his starting point in Fayetteville, North Carolina. He had resigned himself to life after baseball. Nobody even called asking him to take one of those nebulous jobs known as "consultant." He felt wasted. Then one night, the telephone rang.

It was the Florida Marlins calling, and we start from there. It was something out of fairy tales.

When the Marlins hired him on May 11, 2003, the team was wilting in last place in the National League East, six games in oblivion. Naturally there were nay-sayers who threw up their hands and yelped, "My God, they've resurrected Methuslah!"

Being 72 years old ain't exactly being dead. There are some septuagenarians younger than some 50-year-olds I know—and some 40-year-olds creakier than some 60-year-olds.

Honestly, the last place John Aloysius McKeon expected to find himself was inside a uniform with a flying fish on the shirt. He had been sitting at home on his farm near Elon College watching a major league game on television about 11 o'clock one Saturday night when the phone rang again. This time it was the Marlins calling one more time. They were replacing Jeff Torborg and could he be there the next day?

It wasn't the first contact. "They had called in the middle of the week and asked me to fly down and meet with them. I'd never met anybody with the Marlins in my life," he said. "We had dinner. We talked baseball. Nothing was said about managing, and I flew back home."

After the call the following Saturday night, he drove to the airport in Greensboro, a few miles from Elon, and caught a plane at six o'clock Sunday morning and was in the Marlins dugout that afternoon. Pretty swift pace in the life of a 72-year-old.

"I was getting tired of watching my grandkids play ball and sitting around watching television, but I had no idea of getting back in the game. Somebody wanted me and that's all I needed."

He didn't consider himself retired, just unemployed since his last season at Cincinnati two years previous. He still had fire in the

Jack McKeon spent three and a half seasons in Cincinnati, balancing the "quirks" of Ken Griffey Sr. and Jr. *David Tulis/AJC Staff*

belly, and like the old warhorse that he is, he was ready, just knowing somebody wanted him again.

McKeon's trail as a manager began at Fayetteville in the Carolina League in 1955. His path since then reads like an American travelogue. He managed places where Greyhound doesn't even stop. One of his stations was Atlanta, the last season of the old minor-league Crackers in haunted Ponce de Leon Park. Once a showplace at its level, now rodents outnumbered the fans.

It was a Minnesota farm team of misfits, one of the worst minor-league teams I ever saw. Yet six of them would later make it to the big leagues: Jim Merritt, a pitcher of merit; Randy Hundley, the catcher; and Joe Nossek, an outfielder, were three of note.

McKeon was ahead of the game as a dabbler. Instead of trudging to the mound to consult with a wobbling pitcher, he used a walkie-talkie to lecture him from the dugout. He was replaced in mid-season and happily took leave of the ghastly scene.

He made his first major-league connection in 1973, when Kansas City promoted him from Omaha, where he worked with a young director named John Schuerholz. His first Royals team finished in second place, and he was in second place again the third year when the Royals decided to replace him with Whitey Herzog. So he shares with Jeff Torborg the desolate feeling of being sacked while the game is on.

Florida is the fifth major-league team he has managed, after Kansas City, Oakland, San Diego and the Reds. One of the agonies of managing the Reds was dealing with the quirks of the Griffeys, Ken Sr. and Jr., though he'll never go into detail.

In between managerial calls, he has worn nearly every front office title there is: general manager, assistant general manager, senior consultant, personnel director, scouting director and scout.

"I've been everything but president and owner of the club," he said, "and I've never wanted to be either."

He has always felt more at home among the troops, in a uniform in the dugout. He is only assured of finishing the season in Florida, but he's just happy to be wanted again, even if thrust into

The president of the minor-league Atlanta Crackers, Bill McKechnie Jr., presents new manager Jack McKeon with his uniform. *Billy Downs / AJC Staff*

McKeon was 72 years old when he piloted the Florida Marlins to a world championship over the New York Yankees in 2003. *Al Bello / Getty Images*

the category with Connie Mack and Casey Stengel as the three most aged managers in the history of the majors.

Well, the way it worked out is beyond something even the Brothers Grimm might have written. In 2003 the Marlins finished second in the division, then beat the Giants in the first round of playoffs. They followed that up beating the Cubs in seven games for the National League pennant, and blowing reason all out of proportion by taking down the mighty Yankees in the six-game World Series, with Josh Beckett, a 23-year-old kid wearing an ill-fitting chin beard applying the final thrust. It was, beyond a doubt, the story of the year in American sports, and who else was manager of the year but Jack McKeon.

"Managing is not that tough. It's sort of like riding a bicycle," he said, dusting off a lapel. "You never forget how."

—JOE JACKSON—

The Truth According to Shoeless Joe

I t was the summer of 1949. I was sports editor of the *Charlotte News* and on the side managed to handle a freelance magazine assignment now and then. Through a contact in Greenville, South Carolina, I got in touch with Shoeless Joe Jackson, who decided it was time, once and for all, to tell his side of the "Black Sox Scandal" of 1919, for which he had been banned from organized baseball for life. As an outfielder for the tainted Chicago White Sox, he had been a central figure in the World Series in which eight members of the Sox had been accused of dumping to Cincinnati, though his batting average against Reds pitching was .375.

Joseph Jefferson Jackson at birth, "Shoeless" becoming permanently attached to his name after a game in his minor league career

Shoeless Joe Jackson and seven of his Chicago White Sox teammates were accused of throwing the 1919 World Series. Jackson was cleared of the charges in court but was still banned from organized baseball.
Photo in the public domain

when his shoes wore blisters on his feet and he had cast them aside. As he ran out a triple in his stockinged feet, a leather-lunged fan cried out, "Run, you shoeless son-of-a-gun!" So the story goes.

Jackson had settled in a modest bungalow west of Greenville at 119 East Welborn Street, in view of Brandon Mill, where he had worked and played baseball as a youth. He ran a liquor store in West Greenville and lived quietly in this typical, tree-lined Southern neighborhood.

Sport Magazine was the pioneer in the field of sports magazines, several years ahead of *Sports Illustrated*, and paid well, considering the economy of the times. Jackson would tell the story of his role in the World Series of 1919 for a fee of $250. I would be paid $250 to write it, and as I have said several times since, we both needed the money.

He had never granted an interview on the subject before and never would again. "This is my story. This is the truth, and I'll let the Lord be my judge," he said.

I drove down from Charlotte and sat with him near a sapling oak in metal lawn chairs on his front lawn. We talked the better part of a day. Never once did he invite me into the house, though at one break he did go into his garage and bring out the bat that he made famous, his "Black Betsy." He even swung it a time or two, and let me have a swing.

We had crossed paths once before, though it was not a moment he would remember. He had been managing the Winnsboro Royal Cords, a team in a tough semipro textile league in South Carolina, 15 years earlier. A friend of mine in Denton, North Carolina, was Max Lanier, a high school classmate, and a promising young pitch-

Joe Jackson and his wife, Katie, pose with their dog, Beauty. Jackson called Katie his "business head." *Thomas S. England / Time Life Pictures / Getty Images*

er—he would later win 108 games and pitch in three World Series for the St. Louis Cardinals. Max had been offered a contract by a team in Rock Hill. He had never been away from home and feared he'd get homesick, so he asked my father if I might go with him. So we, a couple of country bumpkins, took a bus to Rock Hill.

Rock Hill was playing Chester in a game soon after we arrived, and Jackson sat in the stands, scouting the two teams. He was 46 at the time, but still playing as well as managing. I sidled up next to him in the stands, a brash 15-year-old, and spoke with him briefly, surely nothing for him to file away in his book of memories.

As we talked on East Welborn Street that day, he wore a white shirt and tie and held a Panama hat on his knee. He would, at times, look intently over my shoulder as I made notes. This would be his story, you see, "By Shoeless Joe Jackson," as told to me. By requirement, he would read, then sign the manuscript, making whatever changes he saw fit.

He was surrounded in Greenville by a colony of supporters who were still vocal in maintaining his innocence, revered as a persecuted man. He, however, made it clear that he had never raised his voice in protest.

"I had been acquitted of all charges by a 12-man jury in a civil court [in Chicago] and I was an innocent man in the records. I have never made any request to be reinstated, and I have never campaigned to have my name cleared," he said. "This is not a plea of any kind. This is just my story.

"I thought when my trial was over, Judge Landis might have restored me to good standing, but he never did. Until the day he

A stern figure behind the counter of his Greenville, South Carolina, liquor store, Shoeless Joe Jackson lived a moderately successful life after his banishment from baseball. *Thomas S. England / Time Life Pictures / Getty Images*

died, I never went before him or had a representative do so to plead my case.

"The notice I got read that if found innocent of any wrongdoing, I would be reinstated; if found guilty, I would be banned for life. I was found innocent and still banned for life. If baseball didn't care to give me a square deal, then I wouldn't go out of my way to get back in it."

It might be considered peculiar that at the very moment Shoeless Joe was chairman of the protest board of the Western Carolina League. Later, the baseball park where the Greenville farm teams played was named in his honor. The fight to clear his name was still going on half a century later. Surely, he had credentials for the Baseball Hall of Fame. His lifetime batting average was .356. Babe Ruth once said that he copied his batting stance. Ty Cobb had said he was the greatest natural hitter of all time. His vision was so keen that he still had no need for glasses at the age of 61.

One matter he did wish cleared up: the fable of, "Say it ain't so, Joe," presumably addressed to Jackson by a small boy as he left the courtroom in Chicago.

"Charley Owens of *The Daily News* was responsible for that. There weren't any words passed except between a deputy sheriff and me. He asked me for a ride and we got in the car and left. Charley Owens just made up a good story."

After this story was written, I drove back to Greenville for Jackson's approving signature. It was common gossip that he could neither read nor write. That I can neither confirm, nor deny. However, after he riffled through a few pages, he excused himself, then took the manuscript into the house for his wife, Katie, to have a read. Now he had said earlier that Katie had been his banker, his business head. He returned with a signed manuscript, whether it was hers or his, I can't say. I can say that somewhere in the assorted remains of *Sport Magazine*, now out of publication, there must be a manuscript bearing the priceless signature, "Joe Jackson."

A little over two years later, "Shoeless Joe" died. Whatever kind of secrets he kept within, went to the grave with him. The *Sport Magazine* story keeps popping up on the internet now and then, and interrogating people call, asking to know what secrets Joe and I shared that weren't published. None, I can assure you.

— RICHARD PETTY —

A Family Tradition

Richard Petty had the only unlisted telephone number in Level Cross, North Carolina, and probably still has. If there were no Pettys there, Level Cross would be no more than a bucolic dot on the road that runs between Randleman and Greensboro. The major industry is Petty Engineering—in fact, the only industry. There I found Richard and all the Petty kin in the month of December, in the recess between one racing season and the start of another.

Richard, in his trademark sombrero with its snakeskin band and the belt buckle, big as a skillet, was the star, but Lee, the patriarch, was still boss, and make no mistake about that. Petty Engineering incorporated total family involvement, a point that Lee never failed to make. They never put one over on Lee, as the

Racing legend Richard Petty smiles from the garage in 1971, the year he became stock car racing's first million-dollar driver. *Steve Deal/AJC Staff*

19-year-old Richard found out the day he thought he had won his first race at dusty Lakewood Park in Atlanta in 1959.

Richard had wheeled confidently into the smoky winner's circle at the now extinct track, floating on an air of victory. Suddenly, beside his car came Lee in his, roaring up and hollering, "Just a minute, there."

Lee challenged the decision, and a recount proved him right. "I want him to win, but when he does, I want him to earn it fair and square." Which Richard did the following year.

I had been there for one other landmark occasion in Richard's career. When he became the first NASCAR driver to win a total of $1 million on the track, his sponsors had a little party for him near Atlanta. Now he had been driving race cars for 14 years, and would race on for another 20, and as he has continued as an owner, he has seen some winners earn almost as much in one day as he did in all those 14 years.

So you drive into the Petty grounds on a crisp December morning. Lee's white frame house is spotless, unpretentious but properly situated and expressing a dominance of the compound. The lawn is trim and neatly manicured. Since he retired from racing, Lee has become addicted to golf, and he's getting in some chip shots in the yard. He still walks with a slight limp, a cruel souvenir from the time he went over the wall in the Daytona 500 in the twilight of his career. After that frightful accident, he lost his desire to race any longer.

"I went back and drove again just to prove I wasn't scared," he said.

Richard Petty leans against the tool of his trade in 1992, the year he retired. Petty hung up his helmet with 200 wins and seven NASCAR championships.
Johnny Crawford/AJC Staff

Lee was proud of the Pettys' racing traditions. "We haven't raced like the others," he said, "the Flock boys, Curtis Turner and all them. We have put back into racing. All they did was take and give nothing back."

Richard was working in the garage, what he called "the old reaper shed." There is no stoppage during the off season. Work goes on, preparing cars for the start of the next run. He has been in New York, taking part in a new feature for the NASCAR boys, the lavish banquet at the Waldorf Astoria Hotel, saluting the points champion of the year. I recalled watching Richard seated in a parlor, dressed out uncomfortably in business attire, being interviewed by some reporters from the New York papers, who were exploring a territory new to them.

Petty Engineering prided itself, to repeat, on total family involvement—mother, brother, cousin, all with their roles. Elizabeth Petty, matron of the family, had once kept books for the operation; now it required a staff of four. Besides their own cars, the Pettys manufactured 15 other cars for the market each year.

"It all blended," Richard said, using a term the Pettys often called on. "Everybody's got a part. It all just blended."

He had been to Daytona Beach driving tests, and to Riverside in California, where the first race would be run the next season.

"We play for the breaks," he said. "Any time they say you're lucky, I always say we were prepared for the situation. Take advantage of the breaks when they come. There's no charity in this business. Nobody's looking to give you something."

When I asked him if he ever played golf with Lee, he scoffed, "Play golf? When would I have time? Our days run seven to five during race season, seven to seven during the building season. We work all week. My only recreation is racing on Sunday.

"Before I was married and dating Linda, I told her I might get home by 10 o'clock, or I might not get there at all. My daddy had me working, and that's all I ever done."

Linda was a local girl. She grew up in the nearby town of Randleman, which is where the Pettys went when they "went to the store." Their children went to school in Randleman, where Richard and Linda met. Linda drove them each day. She was a member of the PTA, a Lady Civitan, and a Cub Scout and Brownie leader in Randleman. She was the family representative in community affairs.

Richard never went to college, but he did take a business course at King Business School in Greensboro. "That's all I needed when I got out of high school, something practical to work into the business."

"I'd like to have seen him go to college," Lee said, "but I never ordered him to do anything. He just sort of followed along. That's the way it was. It all blended."

Richard would win 200 races and seven NASCAR championships before he drove his last in 1992. He was known for his toothsome smile, and it seemed he never turned it off, even when there was nothing to smile about. By this time, his closest call, as he rated it, had come at Darlington, when he hit the wall, but he remembers little of it.

"I blacked out before the worst. But I never had any qualms about getting back into a car again."

Richard Petty strolls through the garage area of Daytona International Speedway in 1999, not as a driver, but as a car owner. *Johnny Crawford/AJC Staff*

He would save his worst for the crown jewel race of the circuit, in the Daytona 500 of 1988, down the stretch in full view of the finish line stands and all the cameras. He went somersaulting end over end, backflips, headstands, so many parts flying that there was little left but Richard and the driver's seat. Surely, we all thought, his luck had run out.

When the emergency crew checked him out, they couldn't even find a scratch. Never lost one of those teeth that were such a part of his personality. When they asked him if he was really in one piece, he said, "My ankle hurts."

Richard Petty had one of the most remarkable careers any athlete has ever had in any sport. Two hundred driving victories!

No driver will come close in any class of racing. Oh, they'll win a lot more money. Last time I looked he was 46th in lifetime earnings, but had a lead of over 140 races over the nearest active driver, Jeff Gordon, who was not even in his rear-view mirror. His record as an owner hasn't kept the pace with his as a driver—disappointing at best—but the race goes on.

And he still has all his teeth, his hair, his limbs, and his photographic trademark, that smile.

—PAUL "BEAR" BRYANT—

Homecoming

"**A**t 5:30 a.m. on New Year's Day, a white Cadillac bearing a Texas license pulled into the dark and empty parking lot behind the athletics offices at the University of Alabama. A tall, bareheaded man stepped out and walked with an easy stride toward the building, gravel crunching under his feet ... Paul [Bear] Bryant was reporting for work at his new station."

This was the opening paragraph of a story in *Sport Magazine* of Bear Bryant's return to Tuscaloosa, and things would never be the same again in Southeastern Conference football. Bryant was completing a cycle that began in 1931, when he arrived on the Alabama campus in a model A Ford piloted by Hank Crisp, line coach and leading head-hunter on the staff of the late Frank Thomas. The Warrior River separates Tuscaloosa from Northport, and all traffic from the west approaches Tuscaloosa over that bridge.

"I'll never forget the first time I crossed that bridge," Bryant said, now ensconced behind the desk in his new office. "I was riding in Coach Hank's old Ford. I had on a pair of green knickers. Every boy had to have a pair of green knickers in those days. I had a little satchel with nothing in it but an extra pair of britches and a pair of shoes and a few other things.

"They still remember around here the day my trunk arrived. It was one of those old-fashioned round-top trunks. It had no lock on it, so my mother had tied a plow line around it to hold it together. When I drove over that bridge the other day, I thought about that."

He was not trying to impress the boss with his early-morning arrival. He was the boss. The day before, he had ceased to be athletics director and head coach at Texas A&M. Now he bore the same titles at his alma mater.

This time his return was a command performance. Alabama football was in deep distress. Alumni were in a stew of unrest. The athletics department had been caught in a riptide of discord. It was an awkward situation. Jennings Bryan Whitmore, also an alumnus, had been head football coach, but he in turn reported to the same Hank Crisp, who was his line coach on the field but the athletics director indoors.

There was only one answer: Get the Bear.

Bryant had weathered some storms before. First, at Maryland, where he was hired out of Navy Pre-flight School at North

A young Bear Bryant answered the distress call from his alma mater, leaving Texas A&M to become the head coach at Alabama. *Hulton Archive/Getty Images*

Surveying the field as his team warms up, Bear Bryant carved an impressive silhouette. *Bud Skinner/AJC Staff*

Carolina, there loaded a bus with 16 players still in Navy uniforms and headed for College Park. It was only a stopover on the way to Kentucky, where he got his feet wet in SEC waters. There was a deeply embedded coach there ahead of him, Adolph Rupp, a basketball icon who ruled the realm. It was an unrestful co-existence.

"Kentucky wins a basketball game," Bryant said, "and he gets a Cadillac. We win the Cotton Bowl game and I get a watch."

Next stop: College Station. The beginning was without gusto. His first team won only one game. There, too, he and the basketball coach, Ken Loeffler, whom he had hired himself, crossed swords. Two weeks after Loeffler arrived, the Aggies landed on probation. Football was the culprit. Loeffler seethed.

"If the NCAA really wants to put the blast on the Aggies, it ought to look under the football table," he said. "It's enough to sicken the strongest stomach."

Still, he would only speak in terms of admiration for Bryant and the way he ran a show. "You've got to respect a man who knows what he wants and is forceful enough to go out and get it," he said. "If he walked in here right now, he'd put his arm around me and he'd say, 'Ken, I wanted to hep [sic] you, but you were talking when you shoulda been listening.' He'd be real southern. A big, impressive fellow like that, you've got to respect him."

The Bryant who sat on the other side of the desk in Tuscaloosa that morning in January is a man of complexities. He can be moody, friendly, effusive, reserved, crafty, politic, mule-headed, dramatic, innocent or pseudo-naive. His personality range is as vast as an artist's. He keeps his moods filed away in his mental index, and he can call on any one of them to meet whatever situation arises.

A former coaching contemporary has said of him, "That Bear, he is a strange and mysterious man."

Perhaps this gives a clue to his stature among his coaching fellows: He was once on the NCAA's probation list and on the National Coaches Association's ethics committee at the same time.

While the rest of the Southeastern Conference quaked in its saddle oxfords at the news of his return, he was most self-effacing about himself. "Isn't it true that you have justly earned this awful reputation as a go-getter of talent?" he was asked.

His reply was a showstopper. "Aw, shucks," he began, wrinkling his brow and grinning shyly, "I probably get more credit for doing less recruiting than any coach in the country. Once in awhile, I'll go see a special boy of some kind, but I don't make over five or six visits a year. I don't do as much of it as Bobby Dodd at Georgia Tech."

"But haven't you washed a few dishes, milked a few cows or drawn a few buckets of well water for mothers of top prospects?"

"Oh, I've done a little of that in my time, but not lately," he said.

The recruiting process that got him from Fordyce, Arkansas, to Tuscaloosa was swift and easy, which he confirmed. Hank Crisp simply walked up to him and said, "Would you like to go to Alabama?"

"I sure would," Bryant said, with instant recall. "It was as quick as that."

Star Bama quarterback Joe Namath listens intently to Coach Bryant in 1963, a national championship season. *Billy Downs/AJC Staff*

Bryant didn't return to Alabama for an increase in pay, so it was reported. "He'd gotten so many letters that said, 'You've got to come back. You're the only man who can do it. Alabama needs you.' Letters from influential friends. He had to go back," one of his close friends assured me.

Then, there was the case of the rise of Auburn, otherwise Alabama Polytechnic Institute, pressing hard on the Crimson Tide conscious. Coach Ralph Jordan had upgraded the pride and rating of the Tigers while Bryant was away in the Southwest. Just the season before, Auburn had been rated No. 1 in the nation by the Associated Press. Oh, did this cut deeply into Crimson Tide pride.

"Nobody gives me credit for sentiment, but I owe a lot to Alabama," Bryant said. "It was like hearing your mother call. They gave me every chance I ever had here. I had to come back."

At Texas A&M, his departure was accepted gracefully. In the campus newspaper it was written, "With his resignation, Texas A&M is no doubt losing the greatest coach in America today."

Even the columnist who had written at his hiring, "He'll give us all a bad name," had seen the light, and wrote mournfully of his departure. "Going home to mama," he'd become a god, he wrote. But, as DeLawd said in *The Green Pastures* of his own exalted position, "Dis heah business uv being God ain't no bed uh roses."

—FRANK GRAHAM JR.—

A Case of Mistaken Identity

The second chapter of the Bryant experience is not a pleasant one. As interviews go, the one we had was brief and barely figured in the situation that developed down the road. I had been to Northport, across the river from Tuscaloosa, to talk with Frank Lary, the Detroit Tigers pitcher, for *Sport Magazine*. Since Georgia Tech was scheduled to play Alabama the next week, I dropped in on practice at Tuscaloosa.

I visited with the team manager during practice and noticed one player not in full gear. "Coach Bryant tells us not to let him wear pads at practice, he's afraid he'll hurt somebody," the manager told me.

That weekend he did.

Alabama head coach Paul "Bear" Bryant leaves his hotel to head to the court-room in 1963 to testify in the case of Wally Butts v. *The Saturday Evening Post.*
Charles Pugh/AJC Staff

The game was played in Birmingham and Alabama would best Georgia Tech, 10-0, but that player, a linebacker named Darwin Holt, would leave his physical mark on the Yellow Jackets. It came on a Georgia Tech punt. The Alabama safetyman signaled for a fair catch and Chick Graning, one of the Tech covering players, eased up into a trot. Holt, meanwhile, came at him with a fierce forearm thrust and felled him, but since the fair catch had been signaled, officials also had relaxed and missed the infraction. Alabama was not even penalized.

Graning was taken off the field on a stretcher, and the next day, he looked as if he had been struck by a train. The repercussion in Atlanta was furious and the incident indirectly set off a chain reaction that led to the courtroom months later.

The next fall, *The Saturday Evening Post* introduced a new feature and I submitted a piece on brutality in college football, which was published. In it, I included that incident from the Georgia Tech-Alabama game, and some other incidents in which players had been seriously injured, and named some coaches whose teams had developed a reputation for rough stuff, Bryant included. While none of the other coaches was outraged to such a point, Bryant sued *The Saturday Evening Post* for $500,000, naturally including me as an accessory, and the vitriol began flowing.

Meanwhile, at the University of Georgia, dimly viewing some off-field activities of coach Wallace Butts, the powers that be, in all their wisdom, had deposed him as football coach, but retained him as director of athletics—an incredible conflict of judgment.

His coaching successor, Johnny Griffith, a former assistant, was having mixed success, at best, but Butts was not grief-stricken, though he was head of the department. It developed, later, that he had been telephoning coaching acquaintances around the Southeastern Conference whose teams Georgia was about to play and discussing Griffith's coaching trends, so to speak. One day, from an insurance office of a Butts friend in Atlanta, an agent in the office picked up a phone to make a routine call. What he got was not an open line, but the voice of Butts talking with Bear Bryant about the game coming up with Georgia. Now, there would be no reason to question the athletics director of one school talking with the athletics director of an opponent next on the schedule. But apparently more than mere logistics were being discussed. The agent, realizing what he had cut into, began taking notes, shocked at what he was overhearing.

(Not that Alabama needed any help. Georgia was not a strong team and won only three games that season. Alabama would win the game easily, 35-0.)

The agent who had unintentionally intercepted the call was disturbed. What had he heard? Two coaches having a casual conversation about football strategy, or one coach selling out to the other? Eventually he told a close friend what he had heard, and the friend leaped to the fray. He directed him to a trusted contact—not me— the contact called *The Saturday Evening Post*, and this bird took off in full flight, quite aware that Bryant had a lawsuit pending against the *Post*.

Just a few weeks before, the *Post* had hired a new sports editor to succeed the mild and scrupulous Harry Paxton. The new sports editor was Roger Kahn, well known in sports writing, and he wanted to hit the scene with a splash. He couldn't have asked for a

Toward the end of his coaching career, Bear Bryant scowls from the sideline. Bryant's coaching record stood at 323 wins when he retired in 1982.

New York Times Co. / Getty Images

sharper instrument—two suspect coaches in what he determined to be a surreptitious telephone exchange. A fix, he discerned.

He needed a by-line writer for the story, certainly not me, the object of Bryant's lawsuit. He settled on Frank Graham Jr., whose father had been a distinguished columnist on the *New York Journal-American*, "although I knew nothing about Southeastern football." Here, let Graham take up the telling:

"I was asked to fly to Atlanta and sit in at a meeting during which the *Post's* lawyer from Birmingham would take an affidavit from [George] Burnett (the agent who had accidentally intercepted the Butts-Bryant call). I was to write the draft of an article based on Burnett's affidavit, then the *Post's* lawyers would determine whether it would be published. I was not to let any one else know that I was in Atlanta, not even you.

"I returned to New York and wrote a story based on Burnett's affidavit. Everybody liked the story and said it would be published as soon as certain facts could be checked. ...The next thing I heard when I went to a meeting with various editors was that the *Post's* lawyers had approved the story I had written and they were going to publish it right away; they were afraid of losing a 'scoop' if they waited because the story was now common knowledge.

"Roger Kahn (whether he collaborated with any of the other *Post* editors, I don't know) then wrote a box to precede the article, in which he pointed out that this 'fix' could be compared to the Black Sox scandal. I don't know who put the title on the story."

This was the damning aspect of the situation, not what Graham had written, but this lead-in that likened the action to the Black Sox baseball scandal of 1919, an out-and-out case of game-fixing.

In his trademark houndstooth hat, Bear Bryant "had such charisma. He was just a giant figure," according to Penn State coaching great Joe Paterno.
Hulton Archive/Getty Images

Atlanta Journal editors had made arrangements with the *Post* to release the story at the time of its publication, thus a galley proof of the layout was sent to Jack Tarver, the publisher. When I saw the proof, I picked up the telephone and called the managing editor of the *Post*, a man named Davis Wilcox.

"I've just looked at these proofs," I said. "You're not going with this, are you? There's no resemblance between this case and the Black Sox scandal."

"Well, we decided that if we were going with it, we were going all the way," was his reply.

"You've gone all the way, all right, and then some. I don't see how you can do this."

So much for that. The story was published. It blew up in the *Post's* face. In the trial that followed later in Atlanta, Butts suing the *Post* for damages and the magazine exercised its flawed judgment even further. It retained a courtly corporate lawyer who had little or no experience at the bare-knuckle battling of the courtroom, and lost by a knockout. Not that the *Post* had one chance in a thousand of winning that case, especially since the University of Georgia president denied incriminating statements he had made about Butts, and Griffith, trying to save his job, denied statements he had made. They were all running for cover, trying to save their jobs.

As for authorship of the article, it never became an issue, as far as I know, until later, when the *Post* decided to get out without further courtroom acrobatics and settled with Bryant about the article I had written about brutality in the game. Hence, every son of

Alabama, a probably several daughters, concluded that "Frank Graham Jr." was only my nom de plume.

Here, we turn to Frank Graham again: "I am sorry that you have taken a lot of guff on this. ...I hope that no one besides Bryant has ever suggested that you wrote the story," referring to the story Roger Kahn had edited into a "fix."

Wallace Butts, nevertheless, was soon gone from the University of Georgia, took his $300,000 settlement and retired to the more stable field of auto insurance, and found a happiness he had never known making $75,000 a year. His highest salary as football coach had been $25,000.

His role in this situation was not "rigging," or divulging information for gambling. All he wanted was his job back. He wanted Georgia to lose, that Griffith be fired, and his old school saying, "Wally, come back, we've got to have you on the sideline again." Simple as that.

—SAM SNEAD—

An Afternoon with
Slammin' Sam

An interview with Sam Snead was like trying to balance your-self on a highwire. On the flight down to Florida, I kept ask-ing myself, "I wonder what his mood of the day will be?"

He could be as entertaining as a standup comedian, or he could be grumpy and fractious. It was moving time for him, from his home (for eight months) in Hot Springs, Virginia, to his winter retreat in Highland Beach, Florida, perched 21 feet above the sea-side, dwarfed by the towers of condominiums rising on each side. They had driven down, and his wife, Audrey, and son, Jack, were unpacking, so Sam got a pass from the household drudge, perhaps accounting for his good nature.

A playful Sam Snead gives the camera a wink after winning the 1952 Masters Tournament by four strokes over Jack Burke. *Hugh Stovall/AJC Staff*

This was a distant cry from the hardscrabble life he'd experienced growing up in Ashwood, West Virginia—little more than a crossroads. He was the Li'l Abner of the area—a rustic blessed with more than enough athletic skills for one young man. There has probably been no more complete athlete ever on the PGA Tour than Sam Snead—he excelled at football, basketball, baseball, and track before caddying led him to golf.

So here we sat in balmy comfort, looking out over the beach though a picture window, and while a maid vacuumed and Jack assembled his telescope for sea-gazing, we talked until we had filled nearly three recording tapes.

"I won the West Virginia Open with a round of 61, and I set out on the tour with Johnny Bulla in a 1936 V-8 Ford, leaving behind Orville Welch, the six-foot-six center [I always outjumped him. His feet left the floor but his head never seemed to get any higher.] and ol' Ben Long [He was all bones and knobs and it hurt to block him.]."

He would win his first tour tournament in Oakland in 1937, and the story has been oft-repeated of his surprise when he was shown receiving his check in a picture in *The New York Times*. "Well, I'll be damned, how'd they get that picture? I never been in New York in my life."

"The Masters wasn't thought very much of in those days. I was playing in the Greensboro and I'm was with Fred Corcoran when I get this invitation and I'm not going down there."

But Corcoran, his clever agent, prevailed. "He gets me a practice round with Bobby Jones, so he charters this little old single-engine plane to fly us to Augusta. The pilot had to use a road map to find his way.

"I think I shot a 68 playing with Bob, and I played a couple of exhibitions with him later on. He was a good driver and chipper and putter, but weak on his long irons. If you'll check the record, you'll see that the par-threes gave him fits."

Since the subject was the Masters, his "rick-a-lections"—hill country for "recollections"—were triggered.

"I stayed at the Bon Air Hotel the first year, and I had the misfortune to get a room next to this amateur player and his wife, and they fought every night. Jimmy Demaret was always running up and down the hall, just couldn't sleep. He had a one-hour pill and a two-hour pill and a blockbuster that finally put him out. He was a walking drugstore.

"He always gave the appearance of being calm, but he was all nerves. Walter Hagen was another one that never slept any."

Winning the Masters didn't come swiftly. He sat on the lead Sunday afternoon in 1939 when he thought he had it won.

"There was nothing I could do but sit and wait for Ralph Guldahl to come in, and he beat me by a stroke."

In 1949, it came his time. "I don't remember too much about the first time I won. I remember it was the first year they had the green jacket. Johnny Palmer was leading after the third round, and he was playing right behind me with Jim Turnesa on Sunday. I see him knock it two feet from the hole on number 11, then I went to work. I finish 2-4-4-4-3-4-3. I don't think that course ever played any tougher."

Sam Snead, the second-round Masters leader, marks his scoring form after gaining a two-stroke lead over old foe Jimmy Demaret. Snead eventually lost the 1957 tournament by three strokes to Doug Ford. *Ryan Sanders/AJC Staff*

During the ceremonial start of the 2000 Masters tournament, Byron Nelson (left) and Sam Snead (right) observe a moment of silence for recently deceased Gene Sarazen. *Curtis Compton/AJC Staff*

It wasn't Palmer whom he trumped in the end, it was his close friend Johnny Bulla, who finished tied for second with Lloyd Mangrum.

He won again in 1952, by four strokes over Jackie Burke, and in 1954 it came down to a playoff against Ben Hogan. Billy Joe Patton, the North Carolina amateur, had drenched his chances when his approaches found water on both the 13th and 15th hole. On Monday it came down to Snead and Hogan in an 18-hole playoff, and here, Snead called on his memory of the match, 18 holes in a row.

"This fellow who says he wrote a book about the Masters came up to me at the PGA tournament a year ago, and he starts talking to me about the playoff. He says, 'Hogan never missed a green and you missed five.'

"I told him, 'You don't know what the hell you're talking about.'"

A silence fell over the room. Only sound was that of my tape recorder whirring. Sam re-positioned himself in his chair, as if preparing to activate his recall. Then he began, recounting this round of golf that had been played 21 years before.

"The first hole, we're both on the green in two and two-putt. The second green, I'm on in two and Ben's in the bunker. ..."

On he went, calling up every shot through the entire round, into the 18th green. "Well, there's no sense trying to be a hero now, so I just dog that thing up to the hole and tap it in and I win by one stroke."

It was a monologue that took probably a half-hour. I didn't dare open my mouth, fearful of destroying the spell.

As was tradition since 1984, Sam Snead hits the ceremonial shot to open the 2002 Masters Tournament. Sadly, it would be his last Masters; Snead passed away just over a month later. *Curtis Compton / AJC Staff*

That would be Snead's last Masters championship, but he played on until, at one time, he had played more rounds than any other participant.

His main caddie was a chap named O'Brien, and he and O'Brien had a special relationship. Sam frequently interpolated his conversation with sudden observations, which he did as he spoke of near disaster on the 12th hole, playing the semi-climactic Sunday round on which he and Hogan tied.

"I put my ball in the water on twelve, chipped up and got down in four, and it wasn't looking good. I told O'Brien, my caddie,

'Well, we ain't lost it yet.' [You know, that sucker had 18 children!]" That was Sam, on a loose rein.

Well, it was back to reality. His gardener had checked in. Sam wanted to talk to him about the cinch bugs in the St. Augustine grass. The compressor on the air conditioner had rusted out. One of the awnings had developed a sag.

That covered, he walked me down toward my car, when he suddenly decided he wanted to show me some of his fishing trophies. He kept them in a kind of a maintenance shed, in company with a wilderness of fishing tackle. We walked past a trophy case, dingy from the salt air and mildew, and moved on toward one particular mounting in a central position. It was a fish on a pedestal.

"That's a 15-pound bonefish. I caught it on a 12-pound line. That sucker was a record for several years. Ain't that a beaut?"

I took the chance of breaking in on his exhiliration. "Sam," I said, "where is your British Open trophy?"

He'd won The Open at St. Andrews in 1946 and never went back again.

The purse was a pitiable sum, the trip was expensive and it cost him money, and Sam didn't like to spend his own money.

He rummaged around through a corner of the building, stirring up dust and knocking aside one jim-crack after another until, out of the pile came this little jug. He dusted it up and held it up. "There it is," he said. "You think that was worth the trip?"

My trip had been worth it, and so back to the West Palm Beach airport and home. I'd caught him on his good mood day. He couldn't have been more entertaining.

— PETE RADEMACHER —

Real Joe Palooka

Not many fairy tales take place inside the ropes of a prizefight ring. This one did, and it's the only one of its kind. An amateur turned pro challenging the world heavyweight champion—not only that, but he had the champ on the deck in the second round.

Not only that, but the amateur arranged the fight, promoted it and put up the $250,000 purse.

Not only that, but he sold the deal to the crustiest old con artist in the crustiest old game in the world, Jack Hurley. "The sweet science," as the late ringside bard A.J. Liebling labeled the prizefight.

Pete Rademacher was a real life Joe Palooka—no comic strip palooka. He held the Olympic heavyweight championship, slugged

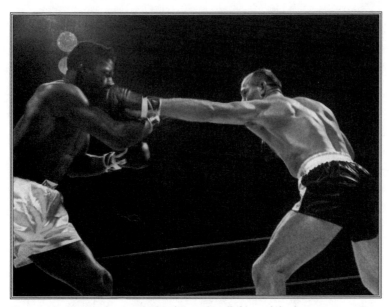

The world's best professional, Floyd Patterson (left), and the best amateur, Pete Rademacher, slug it out at Sicks Stadium in Seattle, Washington.
Hy Peskin/Time Life Pictures/Getty Images

out in the 1956 Games in Melbourne, Australia, when he was Lieutenant Peter Rademacher of the U.S. Army.

Flash forward to near midnight a few months later in the lobby of the Olympia Hotel in Seattle. Rademacher sat and listened to the same old fight stories, one after the other, told by promoter-matchmaker-huckster Jack Hurley, who talked out of the side of his mouth. The next morning they met again, and this time Rademacher did the talking.

"I told him this idea I had of a big fight and all the details. 'You can't do that,' he told me.

"Then I told him I had a plan that would bring it off. 'You're crazy,' he said, then told my wife, 'Take this guy home. He's out of his mind.'"

What Jack Hurley didn't know was that Rademacher had come home from the Olympics to Ft. Benning, Georgia, where he was based, formed a close corporate arrangement with some well-heeled friends in Columbus and gave it the wholesome name of Youth Unlimited. In Rademacher's eyes, his future was unlimited.

"We went to New York and met with Cus D'Amato," Pete said. "I'd never met [Floyd] Patterson, but I was impressed with his manager. The arrangement was Patterson was to get $250,000 off the top. Then I called Jack Hurley one more time, and he laughed at me again.

"Two hours later, he called back begging me to wait. I told him I was with the people who had money and meant business, and if he wanted a part of it, he'd better get his ass to New York. He had trouble getting a plane to New York. My guys had to get back to Columbus, so it took about two weeks to work out the contract."

Then a sudden thought occurred. "What if I win? Of course I'll give him a rematch. And if I lose, well, it doesn't mean I'm through. I'll probably fight some more."

Ten rounds to a decision, if one doesn't go down first.

"My wife cried herself to sleep the night I decided to go through with it. A woman marries a man to be with him, not away from him, and when I went into training, it would be total separation.

Rademacher fought valiantly and sent Patterson to the mat in the second round, with the referee awarding the first two rounds to Rademacher.

Hy Peskin / Time Life Pictures / Getty Images

"It was too late now. It was history, something that had never been done before—world's best professional against the world's best amateur. I thought there was a strong story line there."

Doubly so, for Rademacher. It would be like coming home. "I was raised on an apple farm in Yakima Valley, with five sisters and one brother. First job I ever had was working in a hardware story for 15 cents an hour. I went to Washington State and played football for Forrest Evashevski. Now there was the only man I ever feared."

So when the lights went on at Sicks Stadium that night, Rademacher was the hometown favorite, but not the choice of the bettors. Patterson not only wore the crown, he had another advantage. He was 22; Rademacher was 28. The pro was six years the amateur's junior.

The scene at the old ballpark was electric. Even the New York sports crowd had been drawn to this improbable matchup like candleflies to a light—Red Smith was there, Jimmy Cannon, Barney Nagle and the editor of *Ring Magazine*, Nat Fleischer. Keith Jackson had not yet been graduated to the networks, and he worked the scene for a local television station. Bing Crosby and Phil Harris had interrupted an Alaska fishing trip and sat by ringside. Maxie Rosenbloom was doing a gig in town and came to the show.

Jack Hurley had done a 180-degree turn and was beating the drum, working hard for his 40 percent. "If this guy can't fight a lick, you've got to give him credit for the damnedest promotion job in the history of mankind," he said, thumbs anchored in vest pockets.

Patterson knocked Rademacher down many times during the bout, finally result-ing in a TKO. *Hy Peskin / Time Life Pictures / Getty Images*

The crowd, about 16,000, gasped when Patterson went down for a count of four in the second round. The referee, Tommy Loughran, a classy old light heavyweight, actually gave Rademacher the first two rounds, it turned out later. All came crashing down on the Olympic champion in a flurry in the sixth round, and Rademacher's exploitation crashed with it.

The fight was stopped.

Later, as he met the press in his locker room, he took the stage.

"Gentlemen," he said, "I'd like to make a statement. I'm pleased to have met the champion. I found him exceedingly strong, exceed-ingly quick and exceedingly fair."

At least he won the prize for public speaking.

After the room had cleared, we sat on a couple of stools and he talked of where he might go from there. "I thought I gave him enough fight to think about going on," he said. "I felt right in the ring with him and I. ..." then he broke down in a flood of tears. The great moment had come and gone, and the man who plotted it, arranged it and saw it through, had reached his emotional limit.

Before he got out of town, he had fielded an offer of $20,000 from Madison Square Garden to fight one of four selected opponents. He would fight on. He would win 17 times and lose six.

— OTTO GRAHAM —

A New Purpose

This is another side of Otto Graham, beyond the glory of football, the cheers of thousands, after the parade had passed and his athletics immortality had been established. Ten seasons he played in the All-American Conference and the National Football League, 10 times he quarterbacked his team to the championship game, and seven times won. A pragmatic sort, his differences of opinion with the equally pragmatic coach, Paul Brown, were prominently established, but in the end, when the issue of the greatest quarterback came up, Brown made this magnificent concession: "The best test of a quarterback is where his team finishes. By that standard, Otto Graham was the best of all time."

Case closed.

Years had passed, Graham had moved on through two other stages of life, including three seasons on the other side of the coin. His term as coach of the Washington Redskins netted a record of 17 games won and 22 lost in the late '60s. Now he was going back to Washington again, but this time the mission was far more serious—dealing with life and death. He was honorary national chairman of the Cancer Society of America, and he had earned it the hard way.

Of his return to the capital, he confirmed that his sense of humor was still in place. "I guess it's safe to go back now," he said.

In another phase of his life, Graham had coached and been athletics director at the Coast Guard Academy in New London, Connecticut. "You live in your own world and you read of some fellow having cancer, and you say, 'That's too bad,' and move on.

"Being in the military, I was required to have an annual physical, including a proctoscope, but for two years I had skipped it. Procrastinated. They had this wheel where you roll on your stomach to strengthen those muscles, and one day my tailbone began to irritate me. I went in to be examined and in the process, they found this spot. Had nothing to do with my tailbone. They took a biopsy, sent it off, and sure enough, I had cancer of the rectum. My predecessor had died of rectal cancer, and don't you think that didn't get my attention.

"Klunk! It was a shock. You get it yourself and you become greatly involved. But being an athlete, you always think you can beat it.

"I was sent to Bethesda Hospital in Maryland for colostomy surgery, no complications. Three weeks later I was playing in the

Cleveland Browns coach Paul Brown called quarterback Otto Graham "the best of all time" despite their rocky relationship. *Sporting News/Getty Images*

Otto Graham spent three years as the head coach of the Washington Redskins before returning to the college coaching ranks.

Francis Miller/Time Life Pictures/Getty Images

Bogey Busters Tournament in Dayton. It really doesn't bother your golf game. Be sure to putt on the left side [opposite side of the attached bag].

"Then I had a second operation a month later to relieve adhesions. Complications set in this time—back to the hospital for six more weeks. I really got to the point I wasn't sure I was going to make it. You remember the old news picture of Graham coming out of a Browns game with a mutilated face. Twelve stitches and I was back in. Well, that was nothing, a mere lark compared to this.

"I lost 45 pounds, down to my high school playing weight."

(And here the athlete's pride took a new grip.) "I was due to play with President Ford in the Bogey Busters this time, and I was so severely constipated that my doctor said he had never heard such applause for a bowel movement in a hospital ward."

Well, here the old athlete emerged again. "Five days out of the hospital and I birdied the first hole on my own ball. All those old football thrills were nothing to this. I was never so proud in my whole life."

That he and President Ford and their team won the tournament by a stroke tasted better than winning a football championship. Now he returned to his new mission in life.

"I want to encourage people to have their annual physicals. Cancer draws no social lines. Here I was, the big star athlete—famous and strong; no cancer could bother Otto Graham. How wrong I could be.

"It sounds strange, I guess, but I suppose having cancer is the best thing that ever happened to me. I can't say that I didn't care about people before, but now I look around and I notice people.

Otto Graham was named "Greatest Pro Quarterback of All Time" at a luncheon in New York City on December 6, 1963. *Pictorial Parade/Getty Images*

Spiritually and emotionally, it has opened my eyes. I remember the drive home from the hospital—the lawns, the flowers, the beautiful day, all these things I suddenly began to notice and appreciate.

"It has made me a better person, strange as it may seem. I don't recommend it as treatment to everybody. There has to be a better one."

By this time, Graham had come to see another side of Paul Brown, the coach with whom he'd shared a cat-and-dog relationship at Cleveland.

"If he isn't the greatest coach of all time, all the innovations he brought to the game, he's at least tied for the top.

"When I played for him, I loved him, but, oh, how I hated him. He didn't holler, he didn't scream. He just looked at you with those cold, steely eyes that cut you down more than any kind of words."

This session took place in 1981, 13 years after his first surgery and into the next stage of Otto Graham's life. We were playing partners in a charity golf tournament during Super Bowl Week. His game had slipped a cog or two, but not his zeal for it. We chatted a lot between shots, walking the fairways, prying into private moments that he was now happy to share publicly.

His post-playing career had not developed to the level of his quarterbacking standard. He coached eight college teams against the NFL champions in the College All-Star Game in Chicago. He won twice, and any time the college lads won, it was an upset. He had a creditable career at Coast Guard Academy, and his three years in Washington convinced him it was time to go back to the military. Notably, he was succeeded by none less than the great Vince Lombardi, who soon afterward would die of cancer himself.

Graham lived on until 2003, when he died in December at the age of 82. It wasn't the insidious cancer, the enemy he took on and had long since decisioned, that took his life; or if it was, it never made print.

— BOBBY JONES —

The Making of a Golf Genius

H ardly an angle of Bobby Jones's life has been overlooked by historians plumbing his career in golf, his personal celebrity and his role in creating the Masters Tournament. He was a brilliant man, an academician, broadly educated in subjects ranging from English literature to mechanical engineering. All the more woeful was that he should be stricken with an insidious crippling disease that would eventually take his life.

The curiosity heightened to the point that a movie was made in 2004, based mainly on his career as a golfer, which he brought to an abrupt close after winning the so-called "Grand Slam" in 1930. *Stroke of Genius*, it was called, and while it fell somewhat short of its title, it did re-awaken public interest in Robert Tyre Jones Jr.

In all the historical pursuits of Jones's emergence, his boyhood is generally overlooked. Did he have one? Did he simply spring into life with built-in talent, or how did it all come about?

One day several years ago I sat with him in the office of the law firm that bore his name, Jones, Bird and Howell, in downtown Atlanta, and we talked of the early years—his first knowledge of golf, his first club and the man who gave it to him. By this time, Jones was well in the grip of his ailment and it had been nearly 10 years since he had played his last round of golf at East Lake Country Club, where he had first come upon the game.

"It was a sort of a summer colony in those days," he said. "We lived 'in town' [Atlanta] the rest of the year, but out there in the summer. We 'boarded' with a Mrs. Frank Meadors—a wonderful place. I've forgotten the name of the street, but it was a dead end.

"Her place was built in a quadrangle, and on one side of it there were tents. Some people lived all summer in them. There were other kids there, and we dammed up a little creek and collected turtles and put them in old lard buckets. We used to fish off the dock at the club, and one day I caught a fish and stepped off into deep water trying to bring him in. It was over my head and I almost drowned. The old caddymaster pulled me out.

"There were tennis and basketball courts, swimming of all varieties, golf, of course; everything that a country club was supposed to be. I didn't have any interest in golf, though my mother and father played. One day I was sitting on the steps of Mrs.

Taking a shot in the 1927 British Open, Bobby Jones went on to win the second of his three championships at St. Andrews. *Kirby/Topical Press Agency/Getty Images*

Bobby Jones shakes hands with Atlanta mayor I.M. Ragsdale during the celebration honoring Jones's incredible accomplishment—the Grand Slam. *AJC Staff*

Meadors's place and this man was knocking a golf ball around on the lawn.

"He saw me sitting there and said, 'Little boy, would you like to hit some?'

"He handed me his club, and I whacked at it, but it was too long for me. He pulled an old club out of his bag, a cleek, something like a two-iron, and gave it to me. His name was Fulton Colville [later a substantial figure in Atlanta society]. Dad took the club to Jimmy

Maiden at the pro shop, had it cut down, put a grip on it and I started playing up and down our street with it. You could turn a child loose in the street in those days.

"Later on, we lived out there year-round at several different locations until Dad bought a house on First Street. The kids had dug holes and started playing golf on the street in front of Mrs. Meadors's house. Then they let us start playing on the club course and I had my first match in a junior tournament when I was nine. I played Howard Thorne and beat him and won the championship. I still have the little cup that I won at home.

"I began playing in club tournaments when I was 11. When I was 13, the Southern Amateur came to East Lake and I entered. I drew the oldest player in the field the first round, Commander Bryan Heard from Texas, and I lost, 2 and 1."

East Lake was developing some fine young players, including Perry Adair, a major name in real estate around Atlanta. They were playing an active tournament schedule, and when they traveled out of town, one of the two fathers, Robert P. Jones or George Adair, would do the driving. Then in 1918, young Jones entered Georgia Tech, and earned a degree in mechanical engineering.

"We got up an informal golf team at Tech, Perry and I and two other students. We had the school's blessing, and on one occasion, when we made a trip East to play some of the Ivy League schools, the athletics department even paid our expenses. Two of the members dropped out of school, and that was the end of the golf team.

"When school was in session, I lived at home. I was serious about school and paid little attention to golf."

Affirming this, he eventually transferred his academic attention to Harvard, where he majored in English literature. He was chosen for the Walker Cup team to cross the pond and play the British amateurs. "But it was in the spring of the school year and Harvard wouldn't let me off to go. Yale let Jess Sweetser go, but in my case, it was no hardship. I'd hardly played any at all in the cold Northeast winter."

The Bobby Jones story begins at a house across from Grant Park in Atlanta in March 1902. "I was born in the old L.E. Grant home. Nobody was born in hospitals in those days. Our family doctor, Dr. Kendrick, delivered me. I was an only child. An older brother had died before I was born.

"They didn't think I was going to live for a while. I was sickly as a child, had all sorts of children's ailments. Turning me out on the golf course was probably what allowed me to grow into manhood. At 14, I was five-feet-four and weighed 165. In a year I had grown to five-feet-seven and weighed 175.

"Football held some interest for me, but I was so slow. Another thing, I didn't want some big fullback running over me. I just never was much for bodily contact. After I won the Southern Amateur when I was 15, I knew golf was my game.

"My father and I had a very unusual relationship on account of golf. We'd play two or three times a week, we traveled together and I never regarded him in awe, but with great respect. He tanned my hide only one time, after I fell into the lake and almost drowned. We played together, traveled together and partied together."

As he became an international player, Jones was made an honorary member of every golf club in Atlanta, leading to his acquain-

Gene Sarazen (left) and Bobby Jones were teammates on the 1923 U.S. team, the year Jones won the National Championship of Golf.

Kirby/Topical Press Agency/Getty Images

Legions of fans greeted Bobby Jones upon his arrival in Atlanta after winning golf's Grand Slam in 1930. *AJC Staff*

tance with an intriguing personality, J. Douglas Edgar, the pro at Druid Hills Country Club. Edgar was a remarkable player, an Englishman who made the connection at Druid Hills soon after arriving in the United States in 1916.

"I played a great deal of golf with Edgar. Since he was the professional at nearby Druid Hills and had every Monday off, he and I used to play 36 holes at East Lake during the summer. He was peculiar in a lot of ways, but I liked him very much. I played in several tournaments in which he competed and finished second to him in two.

"One was the Canadian Open in 1919, in which he finished 16 strokes ahead of me. His winning score was 278, which was then a world record for a 72-hole tournament. There was quite a bit of play in the papers about it, but I don't think that was the toughest course I ever played. He would do quite well playing today, I think. He was an inspirational player. He could play all types of shots, but I do not believe he had the driving ambition to concentrate over a long period."

Edgar came to a tragic end on the streets of Atlanta, a mystery that remains unsolved in the records of the police department. It happened late one night as he returned to his boarding house from an evening of bridge in 1923. He was found dying on a sidewalk on West Peachtree Street, either from a knife wound, or from being struck by a speeding car. He had been runner-up in the PGA Championship just three years before—a marvelous talent that was never played out.

Jones spoke of his own condition as we finished our visit. "After golf, I fished for a while with some friends, but my hands became so bad that I had to give it up. I play bridge now and then, and that's about the only contest I have left.

"I make no public appearances, except for some very special event. I can't spend the night away from the conveniences of home. I simply can't dress and undress myself. I go to a dinner with the Spalding Golf people once a year. I visit young Bob and his family once a year, and to the Masters; that about constitutes my travel."

The name of the ailment that devastated his body was syringomyelia. His last appearance at the Masters was in 1968. By the time he died in December 1971, he had wasted away to a mere 55 pounds.

My memory flashes back to an affair in Nashville, honoring Fred Russell, the revered sports writer in the mid-'50s. As laborious as it was for him, Jones made an appearance, drawing a roaring ovation as he arrived.

Then approaching the steps to the podium, he stood uncertainly, unable to attempt them alone. Two strong, gallant guests stepped down from the podium, one on each side and hoisted him to the table—Jack Dempsey and Red Grange.

—PETE ROSE—

From a Happier Time

In the mind of baseball, there are two Pete Roses. One, the Charley Hustle tearing around the basepaths, every body part involved in devil-may-care pursuit of Ty Cobb's major league record for base hits. Two, there is the Peter Edward Rose standing contritely by Commissioner Bart Giamatti's side, hearing himself banned from baseball for life; then later, sitting at a table on a street in Cooperstown, autographing baseballs for a fee, a figure to be ridiculed besmirching this shrine that he had never been able to crash.

Rose rarely hit home runs. That wasn't what the fans paid to see.

Cincinnati Reds third baseman Pete Rose celebrates his record-breaking 4,193rd career hit on September 11, 1985. San Diego Padres first baseman Steve Garvey smiles behind him. *Photo File/Getty Images*

They paid to see him belly-flop slide into second, crash into a catcher at the plate, play this sandlot game with rugged abandon—to see Charley Hustle at work, or play, as you would.

He played the mercenary game for a few years, leaving Cincinnati for Philadelphia, then Montreal, then back to Cincinnati, and there collected his 4,256th hit. Well and fine, but that was not enough. The thrill was missing, I guess, and gambling—big-time betting—became his act, and that's where the story hangs at this time, as Pete Rose roams about like "The Flying Dutchman," a craft without a port.

It was in happier times when we kept an appointment at Atlanta Stadium one day in 1983. Cobb's record was still down the road, but the man and the record were already seizing his interest. A banker named Mills B. Lane, also such a baseball fanatic that he once stood for the $600,000 that got the Atlanta stadium project underway, had commissioned a sculpture of Ty Cobb making that infamous slide into third base, which cost Mr. Lane another bundle. Pete wanted to see it.

Time had left its treadmarks on his features, homely enough, tough enough, yet noble enough to bring out the good nature in another. He was a Tom Sawyer spirit captured in a 1941-model chassis. He never looked upon baseball as an occupation. He played for the love of it. He arrived in a clean uniform and ten minutes later it was dirty again.

He grew up in Cincinnati, a high school football hero and sandlot baseball star. Heaven to Pete Rose was old Crosley Field, a tumbledown piece of architecture that seemed to have been put together one afterthought after another. There was a time when the only team he would ever play for would be the Reds. It hadn't occurred to him that he might become a chapter in baseball history. The only place he was interested in seeing his name was in *The Post* and *The Enquirer*.

One season he played for peanuts in the stifling heat of Macon, Georgia. Four years later, he led the National League in hits, and his salary was bumped up to $24,000. Astonishing. That was his first taste of real money.

But all that has changed. He now wears a Phillies uniform. "I'd rather have played my whole career in Cincinnati, but once I convinced myself they no longer wanted me, leaving was easy."

He had just posed for a photographer by the Ty Cobb sculpture and he wanted to talk a little about the man. "The Georgia Peach," he said, softly. "He was great, but they tell me he could be mean. Was he?"

"I never saw him play," I said, "but I understand he was tough. I know he was tough in real life."

"You knew him, didn't you?"

I said yes, and that was enough of that.

When Ty Cobb was 42, he made his 4,191st hit, batted .323 in 95 games, and retired. At the same age, Pete Rose will have his 4,000th hit and be looking forward to being 43 and making his 4,192nd hit. The suspicion is that he is playing for the record—perish the thought—otherwise, he would be retired and living easy.

He stiffened a bit. "I'm playing for three reasons. I'm playing because I can still play. I'm playing because the enthusiasm is still there, and the other one is I think I have a chance to play in another World Series.

Baseball great and compulsive gambler Pete Rose watches the Kentucky Derby from the stands at Churchill Downs. *Kimberly Butler / Time Life Pictures / Getty Images*

Pete Rose and Hank Aaron (left) pause after the All-Century Team ceremony before Game 2 between the New York Yankees and the Atlanta Braves on October 24, 1999, at Turner Field in Atlanta. *David Tulis/AJC Staff*

"I'm not playing for the record. But I want it."

He remembers his first hit, it was off Bob Friend of the Pirates, a triple.

When he was a Rose bud, 42 must have looked Neanderthal.

"Naaaah, 42 never looked old to me. I got to see my father play football when he was 42. He was a halfback. He was tough and he was good. You had to be to play in that league. I'm sort of a copy of my father, with an opportunity.

"I had quickness. Never had great speed. I knew how to run the bases and I still do." The most bases he ever stole in the big leagues was 20, when he was 38.

Condition is something Rose is always in—doesn't drink, doesn't smoke. "I never saw my father take a drink or smoke or argue with my mother." He laughed. "My kids never saw me take a drink or smoke a cigarette, but I miss on the third."

Rose's clashes with Karolyn were historic, and they were divorced two years ago. What he misses most about Cincinnati is watching his 13-year-old son grow into another Rose off the family bush.

"He is some hitter. I never saw a kid hit that good. The only good thing about the strike last year was that I got to watch him play a little," Pete said.

So this is the man who would replace Ty Cobb at the top of the hit list. He had been impressed, seeing the Felix de Weldon sculpture of the sliding "Georgia Peach." He looked at it with a peculiar air of respect, then put his voice of approval on it.

"Pretty darn good slide," he said.

—BEN HOGAN—

The Hogan Touch

Ben Hogan sat behind the desk in his office at the AMF Ben Hogan Company. It was of modest proportions, fronting a sprawling production plant, located on West Pafford Street in a light industrial area, across the railroad tracks, in Fort Worth. A tan, four-door Eldorado sat in the parking lot.

Ben was cordial, though there was no reason to be tense. A few years earlier, he had been offended by an item in one of my columns about how he had made a contract with *Look Magazine* to reveal the "secret of his swing," and then unwittingly pitched the same "secret"—which was identified as pronation—to *Life Magazine*. *Look* had paid him a fee of $25,000. *Life* paid him nothing.

Ben Hogan patiently waits his turn during a match against Sam Snead at Houston Country Club. *Donald Uhrbrock/Time Life Pictures/Getty Images*

Peace had been made long since, and the matter was never brought up. He knew the subject was to be one of his favorite ones, the Masters Tournament, and he welcomed me with a big smile and motioned me to a chair.

He wore a white shirt and tie, and his jacket hung on a rack behind him, business attire all the way. He had a luncheon to attend later.

As I placed my pocket-sized tape recorder on the desk, the parameters were quickly established. "No tape recorders," he said. "I don't talk into those things."

Down the road, he said, you never know when somebody is going to pull some seemingly harmless sentence off the tape and use it out of context. At least that was the premise; though I heard later that Hogan was quite fearful that something he might say would be put to commercial use.

At the age of 63, he hadn't played competitive golf in several years. He was now the executive Ben Hogan, just a few days before introducing a new line of clubs bearing his name.

They say that he once had tested a new line of clubs turned out in the plant behind him, found them so unsuitable to his delicate touch that he had them all destroyed. A most meticulous man was he.

A few years earlier, while he tuned his game for the Masters at the Seminole Club in Florida, I had walked a round with him. He had shot what appeared to me to be a quite solid score of 70.

"I hit two good shots all day," he said glumly.

Hogan had grown up in the town of Dublin, population about 3,500, 90 miles southwest of Fort Worth. "I'll tell you about

Many golf historians consider Ben Hogan's swing to be among the best ever.
Loomis Dean / Time Life Pictures / Getty Images

Dublin," he said. "It used to have three banks when I was a kid. Now it has one."

The Masters had always been an easy topic for him, a quite special event to him. "Part of it was Bob Jones," he said. "An invitation to the Masters was an invitation to play in the same tournament with him for several years, until his physical condition took him off the course. Augusta National had all those things that make a tournament great."

Hogan had played first in 1938, but played poorly. Then he lost a playoff in 1942 to Byron Nelson, with whom he had caddied at the Glen Gardens course in Fort Worth.

"I was naturally left-handed, but the only clubs I could get were right-handed and I started out playing cross-handed. I finally just had to overcome it by force."

For the longest time it seemed that some cruel fate was conspiring against him at Augusta. He finished second twice, including the playoff loss to Nelson, and fourth twice before finally breaking through in 1951. Then in 1953 came the year of what some called at the time, "The Perfect Masters."

Hogan didn't just break the tournament record that year; he crushed it by five strokes. Gene Sarazen said his record would never be broken, though in time it would be, first by a developing Jack Nicklaus in 1965, then by Raymond Floyd in 1976, and again by the rookie Tiger Woods in 1997.

"I've been debating what four rounds by a single player were the greatest I ever saw for 30 years. Today I got my answer," Sarazen said when all the smoke had settled on Sunday.

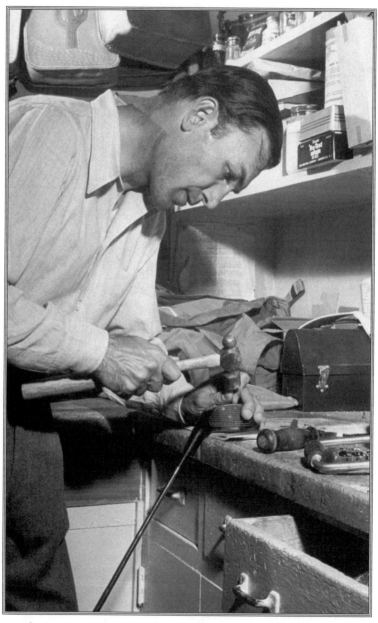

A perfectionist in every sense of the word, Ben Hogan meticulously crafts his clubs. *Martha Holmes / Time Life Pictures / Getty Images*

In the course of the four days, Hogan and Ed (Porky) Oliver, who were co-professionals at the same club in Palm Springs, were paired in the third round, and on that Saturday those two played one of the most combative rounds in any Masters. Oliver broke on top, but by the turn Hogan was up by two strokes. After 14 holes he had a six-stroke lead, but with an eagle at 13 and three birdies in the last four holes, Oliver came within a stroke of catching Bantam Ben. They finished 66-67. Hogan finished off his "perfect" Masters with a round of 69 on Sunday for 274 and a five-stroke lead on the porcine one.

In the aftermath of it, Hogan himself added a museum kind of testimonial to it all when he said, "That is the best I've ever played for 72 holes."

We finally moved on to the year of his last Masters, 1967, and one more glorious turn around Augusta National. It would be the kind of round reserved for a hall of fame. After turning in even par on Saturday, Hogan came around the back nine in 30 strokes, and at every green, he was greeted by a standing ovation.

"You talk about something running up and down your spine," he said, "that round of 66 ... well, it's hard to describe my feelings. I'd had standing ovations before, but not nine in a row. I think I played the best nine holes of golf in my life those last nine holes."

It was followed, disappointingly, by a closing round of 77 on Sunday, and Hogan never played in another Masters. He had made a habit of "going into training" at the Seminole Club in Palm Beach, preparing for Augusta.

Then came the spring that he gave his game the final test and worked arduously to get into condition for the tournament, but at

Ben Hogan and his wife, Valerie, pose at the British Open.
Carl Mydans / Time Life Pictures / Getty Images

the end of a week at Seminole, he and his wife, Valerie, headed for Fort Worth, not Augusta. His game did not come up to his demanding standards to put on public display. It was over.

In 1952 it had been Hogan who suggested to Clifford Roberts, the austere tournament chairman, that a dinner of champions might be a nice idea. "Just sitting around shooting the bull, those of us who talk the same language. To talk of old times and great moments, an evening of fellowship," he said.

It was a sell. The tradition still goes on. On Tuesday night before the tournament, past champions and some officers of the club gather and "shoot the bull" and "chew the fat," as they say. The defending champion selects the menu and picks up the tab.

After he withdrew from competition, Hogan never went back for the champions dinner. The idea of standing around like a museum piece, signing autographs and shaking hands, had no appeal for him. I suggested that it would a monumental moment should he return to the scene, stand under the great oak and be seen once again.

"They've invited me to get involved, but I haven't had time. I will, one of these days. I'll get back."

He never did. Once the battle had been fought and his war was over, so was his interest in returning to the site, though to him, it was "the greatest tournament in the world."

As an aftermath to reminiscences of the Masters, the matter of Hogan and his experiences in course design came up. It may answer a question sometimes asked: Did Ben Hogan ever design a golf course?

Not alone. At the time of this visit he was becoming involved in a project strongly encouraged by his wife. He had bought an interest in some property north of Fort Worth and together with Joe Lee, the distinguished architect from Florida, noted for resort courses, had worked out plans for a golf club to be known as The Trophy Club. Valerie also contributed the name.

I drove past the property later on the way to visit with Byron Nelson, and it looked to be waiting for a golf course to be laid across its breast. As it turned out, Hogan never stayed the route. Either he and Lee tripped over a grievance, or Hogan simply lost interest. The Trophy Club is still there. There is a touch of Hogan in it somewhere, but that's a close as he ever came to course architecture.

— DENNY McLAIN —

Life in the Fastlane

F or two seasons in the late 1960s, the most dominating pitcher
in the American League was Denny McLain.

In 1968, when he won 31 games for the Detroit Tigers, he was
voted both the Cy Young Award as the outstanding pitcher and the
American League award as Most Valuable Player. He won 24 more
games the following season, but there took hard turn onto the
rocky road to catastrophe.

This was not so much a live interview as it was the sad autop-
sy of an earlier one. Even later, while McLain was incarcerated in a
prison in Alabama, we made connection again. He was ready to be
interviewed one more time, but he had an appeal pending, and

Dominating Tigers pitcher Denny McLain winds up during the World Series against the St. Louis Cardinals at Busch Stadium in October 1968, the year he won 31 games for Detroit. *Focus on Sport/Getty Images*

would I be kind enough to wait until it had run its course. That was the last direct contact we had.

By the way, as you will note below, he once played the organ well enough to have made one album. I have a copy in my vast musical library.

⁂

The sign was still out front long after the proprietor had pulled stakes and the joint had gone dark. It hung under the marquee on the Ponce de Leon side of the old Georgian Terrace Hotel, the neon tubing empty of color.

"Gaffer's" was the name Denny McLain had put on his lounge, tavern, bistro—call it whatever you would—another watering hole. It was located on the lower level of a once ornate hotel desperately trying to hold on to the last vestige of flossier times.

So, in a sense, was Denny McLain. His vestiges were threadbare even then, but you had to say this for the guy: He never saw a cloud in the sky. There was a pot of gold out there somewhere, if only he could find the rainbow.

Denny was the kind of guy who always figured he had the answer, even when he wasn't sure what the question was. He figured nothing could get at Big Denny. He was too smart. He had too much on the ball. He was Dennis Dale McLain, world's greatest pitcher, and if he was down, he'd be back up there.

It didn't matter that his fastball was gone, he was ingloriously out of condition, his earned-run average was about the size of his waistline, and he was unemployed. Denny had the conviction that, once a king, always a king—once the greatest, always the greatest.

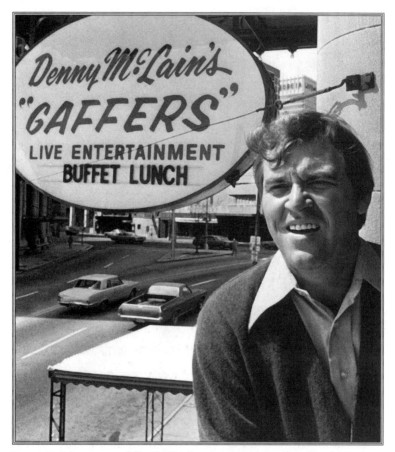

Denny McLain unsuccessfully tried his hand at nightclub ownership in Atlanta. "Gaffers" failed, and McLain's demise was not far behind. *AP/WWP*

He didn't realize it then, but he had pitched and won his last major league game in Atlanta on August 8, 1972. He would never make it into another season. "Gaffer's" was his next act.

He would become the world's next great nightclub operator. Sherman Billingsley, Billy Rose, Toots Shor all in one irresistible personality. (His choice of name for the place was out of character. A "gaffer" is an old man.)

Denny had developed another talent on the side, playing the organ above hobby level. He would have made it in the average Holiday Inn cocktail lounge. So it was expected that he would entertain in his own parlor, offering himself as his star attraction. After all, a recording company had produced one album.

During the World Series in 1968, he had played wildly into the night for kicks in the lounge of a St. Louis hotel where the Detroit Tigers put up.

No organ playing for him, he said to an interviewer, namely me. He would be the affable meeter-and-greeter of the place, not the organ grinder.

I don't know when "Gaffer's" took the gas, but I drove past one day and it was shut tight. Denny was gone. He had had one more spring training—a half-hearted appearance. The Braves had invited him, the courteous thing to do for the once-greatest pitcher. It was an exercise in futility, considering his condition, or lack of it. Even in his myopic state, that was one thing he could see clearly.

What he couldn't see was what a baseball derelict he was becoming. He'd been working at it since he was at his very peak. He bought jet planes he couldn't pay for and learned to fly. He had a brief vision of himself as an airline entrepreneur. He bought automobiles he couldn't pay for. He bought real estate he couldn't pay for. He tried to pay off his debts with his signature, which was worth something only on a baseball.

A classic pitching arm had come attached to a totally undisciplined character. Not since Lefty Grove had gone 31-4 in 1931 had there been such a season pitched in the major leagues as McLain's in 1968, when he was 31-6. Three season later, he was 10-22.

In between, he had had one season of 3-5, but that was the season he did time in Commissioner Bowie Kuhn's cooler. He'd run into trouble with "the mob," he'd doused a reporter with a bucket of water, he'd been caught carrying a gat, but otherwise checked out as an exemplary citizen.

Atlanta was his last stop in uniform. Eddie Robinson, the Braves general manager, gave up Orlando Cepeda (now in the Hall of Fame) to get him, and McLain paid for himself in one day. Over 50,000 paid to watch him make his first start, which didn't last long. The three games he won for the Braves were strugglesome. He was through, washed up, and he wasn't 30 yet.

After life with "Gaffer's," McLain turned up in Memphis, running a minor league team. The problem there involved missing funds, and he hit the road again. He managed to stay out of black headlines until the big storm broke over his head.

This time, he was hit with the book: extortion, bookmaking, drug smuggling, and a few coattail charges. He was hauled in for indictment, which made for heavy lifting. In 1968, he had weighed 186 pounds. In 1984, he had filled out, as they say, to 300 pounds. He could have played the blimp at the county fair. He was a tragic, pathetic, grotesque figure—all three. His was a textbook case of self-destruction.

His pitching companion in Detroit was Mickey Lolich, who picked up the Tigers and turned them around in that World Series of 1968. Lolich was of rather rotund construction even then, but he maintained pitching condition long enough to win 217 games. When retirement time came, he exited gracefully, went back to Detroit and opened a doughnut shop.

Overweight and out of shape, Denny McLain's last stop as a pitcher was with the Atlanta Braves in 1972. *AP/WWP*

One morning last week, Mickey Lolich arose before dawn, as usual, and went to the shop to see that the doughnuts were properly prepared for the day. That same day, in Tampa, Florida, the jury was selected to hear the case of Denny McLain—seven women and five men.

— RED GRANGE —

The "Ice Man" Remembers

His Roots

B y this time, Red Grange had retired to a burgeoning development called Indian Lake Estates, a few mile east of Frostproof in Florida. His was a modest home on a canal, and one home in the area looked about like all the others. He had been in the insurance business, but retired to Florida after a heart attack.

I had met him a few times before, most memorably in Mobile, Alabama, at the Senior Bowl Game. He and Lindsey Nelson, the major broadcast team in football in those days, were working the game.

This happened to be the day that Bear Bryant had announced he was suing *The Saturday Evening Post* for libel, and it being Alabama

All-America football player Harold "Red" Grange jumps for the ball during a promotional photo shoot for the 1926 American Football League New York Yankees. *American Stock/Getty Images*

and Bryant being Bryant, the story was splashed across the front page of the afternoon paper in Mobile.

The issue was an article I had written in a series the Post had just started, and it dealt with brutality in college football. Bryant figured in it prominently, but that's neither here or there. Only that Grange, in a quiet voice, said that Bryant was not a coach he held in high esteem, and let it go at that.

Now it was spring and major league baseball teams were in preseason training. I had called Red for a visit and he had invited me over. We sat on the deck overlooking the canal. My young son played about our feet, and comported himself quite admirably while we talked. What we talked about had little to do with football, but mainly the subject of C.C. Pyle, a flamboyant promoter long since swallowed up in the maw of "Roaring Twenties" lore.

Pyle was a remarkable symbol of that age, and it was pure happenstance that he and Grange crossed paths while Grange was in his prime at Illinois. Pyle operated two theaters in Champaign, and Grange met him as he walked out of one of the theaters one night. Pyle is significant in the story of Grange, for it was he who signed Red to a contract and set him off on his spectacular career in pro football.

"After my last college game in 1925, I went down to a movie, and the theater operator told me, 'Mr. Pyle would like to see you in his office.'

"When I walked in, he said, 'How would you like to make $100,000?'

"I said, 'Who do I have to kill?'

In 1987 an aged Red Grange stands in front of a painting of himself made by his Illinois coach, Bob Zuppke. *AP/WWP*

"Well, he had made arrangements with the Bears for me to play my first pro game on Thanksgiving Day. He got mad at the NFL when the league wouldn't give him a franchise, so he organized the American Football League in 1926. The two leagues merged the next year.

"He was one of a kind, a Beau Brummel of his time. He may have invented the term, 'going first-class.' He always said, 'It's not how much money you've got, it's how you look.'

"He drew up a plan for the first covered stadium, with a dome that could be closed or opened. It was set on electric rollers and cost about a million dollars, anything to eliminate the problem of weather. He was way ahead of his time.

"He put on this cross-country foot race, from Los Angeles to New York, and runners came from all over the world. They called it the 'Bunion Derby,' $100,000 to the winner. He had me along as a sort of sideshow attraction, I guess. It was a major news event. He bought a bus and had it specially equipped, with kitchen and toilet. We'd go around 50 to 70 miles a day. I was with him as far as Chicago, but I'd had enough. It was like a carnival in every town where we stopped. Some of the runners would go crazy. Three hundred started and 55 finished. A policeman from Oklahoma named Andy Payne won it. Pyle made money the first year, but lost it all the next year, and that was it.

"He was a dynamic fellow, a real operator with a thousand ideas. He was married seven times, three times to three former wives. He ran through three or four fortunes and died in 1939, at the age of 56. He used me, but it made no difference. If Charley

The "Wheaton Ice Man" was better known as the "Galloping Ghost," thanks to his phenomenal ability to run the ball at Illinois. *New York Times Co. / Getty Images*

took me for anything, it was worth it to have met him. I wouldn't have lived if I hadn't known him."

Throughout a casual afternoon with Red Grange, on the deck of his home, we had talked little of his sensational playing career, such as the game in 1924, when he scored four touchdowns in 12 minutes against Michigan on the day Illinois's Memorial Stadium was dedicated.

I remembered that W.C. Heinz, the great New York writer, had done a story on having dinner with him one night in Syracuse, where Grange and Nelson had a broadcast assignment. He told of how he came to land at Illinois.

Recruiting had not been honed to the fine science that it is today, if "science" be the proper term. Grange had grown up in Wheaton, Illinois, where he worked on an ice wagon during the summer, thus becoming known later as the "Wheaton Ice Man."

He wanted to go to Illinois because it was the thing to do in the state, go to Illinois and play for the great Bob Zuppke. "There were no athletic scholarships in those days, and it was the cheapest place for me to go," he said. "In May of my senior year in high school, I was there for an interscholastic track meet, and had just finished the broad jump when Zup came over.

"He said, 'Where are you going to college?'

"'I don't know,' I said.

"He put his arm around me and he said, 'I hope here. You may have a chance to make the team here.' That was the greatest moment I'd ever known."

And he did, and the rest of the story is legend.

Heinz asked him if he had any memorabilia from his career at Illinois.

"No," he said, "I don't have anything. I don't even have an I-sweater."

They walked a few steps, Heinz wrote, then Grange paused and said, "You know, I'd kind of like to have an I-sweater now."

If he ever got one, I never knew. He was never one for collecting things. During the day, Mrs. Grange ("Muggs" to Red) came out with a small gold-plated medal. It was the medal Grange had won in the broad jump the day he met Bob Zuppke.

—TED WILLIAMS—

"The Kid" Sizes Up Big-League Hitters

Over these many years, dating back to 1945, I managed to connect with Ted Williams, the great Boston Red Sox outfielder, at various stages of his life, in various ventures and adventures. Herewith:

1945—When he was in Marine Corps flight training at Bronson Field, a wing of Pensacola Naval Air Station in Florida.

1950—In Tampa, at a spring training game between the Red Sox and Cincinnati at Plant Field, when he aimed a glob of spit at jeering fans after hitting a home run. Those were days when teams used hotel rooms as changing rooms. I pursued Williams back to the Floridan Hotel, where his roommate, Billy Goodman, a fellow North Carolinian, eased the tension for me.

Many people believe Ted Williams to be the best hitter of all time. *TSN/Icon SMI*

1961—When he was making his debut with Sears, Roebuck as a consultant executive in the merchandising giant's sporting goods field. He had played his final season for the Red Sox, and disavowed any interest in managing, "Absolutely none."

1969—Eight years later, in the dugout at Pompano Beach, Florida, where he was breaking in as manager of the Washington Senators. He lasted four seasons and quit after the Senators became the Texas Rangers and lost 100 games in 1972.

1987—Then this, when as the featured speaker at the annual midwinter Hot Stove League celebration in Raleigh, North Carolina, and I as his introducer, we shared a suite at the Sheraton Hotel, this last interview occurred. Three hours of Ted Williams all to myself. As you will see, there were times the interviewer became the interviewee. Williams was of a very inquisitive nature.

Ted Williams was talking hitting from a position of total comfort, half-buried in an overstuffed sofa. When Ted Williams talks hitting, it is advisable to listen, as when Bernard Baruch once talked investing from a park bench.

Williams was not the greatest ballplayer that ever lived. All he'd asked was that as he walked down the street, people would say, "There goes the greatest hitter that ever lived." There was never one better.

"It's the hips," he said. "That's the key."

"Jim Rice came to me during the season last year and wanted to know about hitting. I had never talked to Rice about hitting. Let him come to me.

Ted Williams managed the Washington Senators for four seasons but quit after they became the Rangers and lost 100 games in 1972.

Paul Conklin / Pix Inc. / Time Life Pictures / Getty Images

"I told him the hips lead the hands through the swing. He was getting his hands too far in front of his hips trying to pull the ball, and it was causing him to hit ground balls."

It must have worked. In mid-August, Rice had hit only nine home runs. The last month and a half he hit 11.

"The best hitter in baseball today?" I asked.

"The guy from the Yankees," he said, meaning Don Mattingly. "I have to go along with him, but I'm not sure the kid from California (Wally Joyner) isn't going to be as good as any of them.

"Wade Boggs is a good hitter, but he's the Rod Carew type, sprays it around. Oh, what a hitter I thought Dale Murphy was going to be. What a beautiful swing, but he goes after too many bad pitches, especially last season. What went wrong with him?"

"Tried to carry the whole team by himself," I said.

"I hear people say that, but I don't agree. I tried as hard as I could every time I went to bat. That's what you're supposed to do. I wanted to carry the team."

The name of one of the great running backs in the area came up, Charlie Justice of North Carolina, All-American and state legend. The subjects were jumping from one game to another. Williams murmured, "If I coulda run, if only I coulda run, I coulda had some fun."

Ground speed was not part of his game. He stole only 24 bases in his career, but why would you risk a lifetime .344 hitter stealing bases?

"Tell me some of the great athletes you knew or saw," he said.

I told him I'd seen Jack Dempsey fight, saw Bill Tilden play tennis, saw Shoeless Joe Jackson play baseball (at age 46 in a textile

After retiring, Ted Williams served as a consultant and spring training batting instructor for the Boston Red Sox. *Chuck Solomon/Icon SMI*

league), saw Cy Young pitch (at age 67 barnstorming in the South), knew Red Grange, Bobby Jones, Ty Cobb, and saw Jim Londos wrestle.

"I knew Strangler Lewis," he said. "I asked him to try the stranglehold on me to see if it was really anything. He almost squeezed my head out of shape.

"I met Bobby Jones one time. I saw Rocky Marciano coming out of a hotel one time and I said this can't be the heavyweight champion of the world. He was so small. For my money, Joe Louis was the greatest fighter that ever lived.

"Did you ever see Babe Ruth or Lou Gehrig?" I didn't. But I did see Babe Ruth's funeral. I was in New York the day he was buried.

"I knew them both, but the Babe was was already talking in a croak when I met him. I really didn't meet Gehrig, but I walked up the stairs behind him and I remember I had to slow down because he was already a sick man."

"I knew Ty Cobb well." Here he sat up straight and fire sparkled in his eyes. "Some guy wrote a story that we didn't get along very well. We got along just great. I never had any trouble with Ty Cobb. I think it bothered him that he lived in the shadow of Babe Ruth. He was bitter about that, I think.

"I met Judge Landis. I met Walter Johnson. He was a tall, rawboned kind of man. He was a Congressman from Maryland then and I was 19 years old. I never heard anybody speak an unkind word about Walter Johnson.

"I liked Happy Chandler, he was a players' commissioner. What do you think of Ueberroth?" He paused for a moment, then answered his own question. "Peter Ueberroth, if he stays with it, I think will go down as the greatest commissioner of them all."

Other heroic names of other times flowed through his mind. "I knew Connie Mack, of course. I met Rube Marquard, the left-hander who won 19 games in a row, and it's still the record. I spent a lot of time with Jim Thorpe, when we both worked for Sears, Roebuck. I remember, just watching him move made you know that he was a special athlete.

"I think he liked baseball best because he was proud of his record in the big leagues. He played in a World Series, you know."

It was over two hours later—the sun was fading away, leaving long streaks in the sky—when the Hall of Fame came up. Williams is a member of the Oldtimers Committee and it meets shortly to vote on its 1987 favorites.

"What do you think about Roger Maris, and Babe Herman and Wesley Ferrell?" he asked, but my reply is of no consequence here.

"Babe Herman was a great hitter." Williams has great respect for good batsmen. ("Hitting a baseball is the hardest one thing there is to do in sports," he has said.) "What do you think his life-time batting average is? .324. And he could run. They talk about his fielding, but he said, 'You get a reputation early, it never fades.'

"Ferrell won 20 games his first four seasons in the big leagues. And he won more than 20 twice more, then his arm went bad. And he was a fine hitter. He's a tough case. I think he belongs.

"So does Joe Gordon. Look at his record. He had power. He hit home runs, drove in runs and there was no doubt about his glove. I helped Bobby Doerr get in last year, now it's Gordon's turn."

"The Splendid Splinter," Ted Williams, passed away in July 2002 after a long battle with heart ailments. *AP/WWP*

A mellowing factor was detected in Williams, two years away from his 70s. He has taken up tennis with the kind of passion Williams takes up anything.

"I don't fish as much any more," he said. "Tennis is great for conditioning. I'm about an average B-player, I guess."

The 50th reunion of his high school class comes up in San Diego in March, and guess who's going to be there?

"They've invited me for years and I've never gone. I'm going this time and I'm looking forward to it, to see the guys I played baseball with. Yes, yes, I'm looking forward to it."

He lives well. He was the first big league player favored with a deferred-payment contract. He has squirreled away his earnings. Soon he'll take leave of the Florida Keys and establish residence at a development near Homasassa Springs. He has an 18-year-old son at Bates College, a 15-year-old daughter with her mother in Vermont, and the usual concerns of a father, though at long distance. All of these serve to make mellow of a man who majored in swinging a bat and earned his doctorate.

Postscript: None of the players he mentioned has ever been voted into the Baseball Hall of Fame. I never was sure he made good on his pledge to attend his high school reunion. He did indeed settle near Homasassa Springs, where he established a Hitters Museum, there died and the story of his heirs' squabble over his remains became a disgraceful story. The son, John Henry, followed him in death awhile later, victim of leukemia.

—TOMMY LASORDA—

Baseball's Goodwill Ambassador

Any time spent with Tommy Lasorda could easily turn into an interview. Sometimes you never even had to ask a question. You plugged him in and he was off and running on his favorite subjects: patriotism, the flag, the virtues of baseball, the Los Angeles Dodgers and his wife of all these years, Jo.

He was "this great game's" leading missionary, in the hustings as well as bustling cities. No burg was too small. He told once of coming to the rescue of a hamlet in Mississippi named Caledonia, population 821.

"I had a letter from this coach named Smith. I forget his first name. He said that they were trying to raise money for a baseball field at the high school. He'd heard that I'd sometimes make

Dodgers manager Tommy Lasorda celebrates after a win over the Braves in 1985. Lasorda's love affair with the Dodgers has lasted over a half-century.
Rich Addicks/AJC Staff

appearances to help baseball programs raise money for things like this. Would I consider coming to Caledonia and speaking at a dinner to help them build a baseball field?

"Well, I got him on the phone. 'Is this Mr. Smith?' I asked the man who answered. Being a small town, everybody knew the coach. He said, 'Yes, who's this?'

"'Tommy Lasorda,' I said.

"'C'mon, now, who is this, really?'

"'Tommy Lasorda, like I said. I'm calling about your letter,' and it went on from there. He couldn't believe that I'd come to a little town like that and help them develop a baseball program. When it was announced, the thing got so big there was no place large enough to have the dinner in Caledonia, so they moved it into Columbus, the county seat, and the place was overflowing.

"I loved doing things like that to promote this great game. I spend my time selling baseball in any town that wants to listen. I tell them what's right about it, not what's wrong; and a lot of times, it's the team, not the manager.

"One time in Los Angeles, sports writers were writing that baseball was losing interest. They wrote that errors were killing us. Yet, while Lakers were playing the Celtics one night, we still drew 32,000. We pitched Fernando Valenzuela the next night and drew 53,000. I called this writer and I said, 'See how the game is losing interest? And we haven't made an error in seven games.'"

"Six, Tommy," one of his coaches corrected him.

"OK, we haven't made an error in six games." Tommy was very flexible, except when it came to four things: "love of God, my wife, the United States and family, and life as a Dodger.

After retiring from managing in 1996, Tommy Lasorda took a post in the Dodgers' front office. *John Cordes/Icon SMI*

"I borrowed $500 to get married in 1950, when I was pitching in Greenville, South Carolina, an Italian Catholic and a Southern Baptist. It was the best investment I ever made. Fifteen years later I'm managing a rookie team in Ogden, Utah, for $6,000 a year, then up to triple A, then the Dodgers, and I still haven't paid back the $500.

"Nobody knows how happy a man can be no matter where he is, and I'm no more happy now than I was when I was managing a Dodger farm team, making $6,000 a year in Ogden. Try to believe that."

Lasorda preached "Dodger Blue" and the "Great Dodger in the Sky," and he was not beyond stretching exaggeration to the breaking point. "They say that when nine people died in Los Angeles last year, their last words were, 'Did the Dodgers win?'"

Well, did they?

"As luck would have it," Lasorda said, "they did."

On the Dodgers' trips into Atlanta, it became a sort of ritual that I'd have Lasorda to lunch at my courtly old downtown club. He never disappointed elder members, bankers, brokers, and professors who were not shy about coming to the table to be introduced. One day a fellow, obviously a baseball buff, asked that Tommy replay an incident he had read of in some sports publication, "The only time you ever threw at a batter," he said.

Tommy was delighted, for it was one of his favorite stories. The Dodgers were playing the Giants in an exhibition game and Lasorda was on the mound when an outfielder named Buster Maynard came to bat. He flattened Maynard with his first pitch, then his second pitch, then a third before Maynard grounded out.

Armed with his winning smile, Tommy Lasorda is baseball's unofficial ambassador. *John W. McDonough / Icon SMI*

"After the game, Maynard was waiting for me outside of our clubhouse. I thought he was going to punch me, but he had this puzzled look on his face.

"'Why are you throwing at me, Lasorda? I never saw you in my life until today.'

"'When I was a kid and the Giants were playing the Phillies, I told him, I was waiting outside the clubhouse in Philadelphia and asked you for your autograph. You brushed me off and said, 'Get away from me, kid,' and I never forgot it. This was my chance to brush you off.'"

Another dining experience took place in New York, during a World Series between the Dodgers and Yankees. The teams had switched from Los Angeles to New York and after flying in, I had walked down the street to an Italian restaurant on Second Avenue. The walls were lined with pictures of athletes and entertainers, a favorite hangout of Lasorda's when he was in New York, as it turned out. I was reading a newspaper, waiting for my order when Lasorda, his wife and a group of Dodgers came in and were seated at a bank of tables across the way.

Tommy came over and said, "Why don't you come join us?"

"I've already ordered, Tommy, and I'll just read my paper and get back to my room. But thanks."

About this time, the waiter appeared with my order of linguini and white clam sauce, naturally. Tommy never said a word, picked up the order, walked across to his table, put it down at a vacant spot, then said, "Now will you come join us?"

About a half-hour later, Frank Sinatra walked in and joined us, took a seat next to me. He had been rehearsing for a big show that was coming up at Madison Square Garden and Lasorda had made arrangements for him to join his party. About the only thing I remember from the occasion was that Sinatra, upon learning of my line of work, said, "This is the first time I ever had dinner with a newspaperman," which, of course, was not an original line. I could truthfully say it wasn't the first time I'd had dinner with a crooner of such stature. I'd had dinner with Bing Crosby before, several times.

Any time Tommy Lasorda was in the vicinity, it was an occasion, or it soon became one. There has never been another who loved his country, his team, his game and his wife more, and thereby hangs a tale half told.

—TED TURNER—

Media Mogul

Over the years, from billboard advertiser to yachtsman to television pioneer, Ted Turner has been the most entertaining subject in the South. Bar none. One morning in a hotel in Tokyo, I
turned on the television and there was Teddy boy. Same thing on a
visit to London. I have written of him from Moscow, from St.
Petersburg, from Rhode Island, from New York, from a Federal
courtroom, from the muskily odorous interior of a baseball clubhouse, from the deck of the yacht he would pilot to victory in the
America Cup.

He could be quite handy with quotes from the Bible, as on the
day I talked with him early in his ownership of the Atlanta Braves.
He was becoming quite famous now.

Ted Turner squeezes a stress ball during an interview in his CNN office penthouse in 1996. *Phil Skinner/AJC Staff*

He said, quoting from Paul's letter to Timothy, "'I've learned that whatever state wherever I find myself, therein to be content.'

"I've always liked what I'm doing. I cleaned latrines in the Coast Guard and I made up my mind to like it. I've dug postholes for billboards for 50 cents an hour. I've smeared paper on those boards and liked it. My ego is not involved. I drive a Chevrolet, ride tourist and shine my own shoes," and he was rolling.

But no so fast there. Soon he traveled in his own plane with his own personal pilot. He moved up from Chevrolet to a luxury vehicle. When the shine wore off his shoes, he simply bought another pair. He married a movie star, then divorced her. He was moving in the fast lane.

Having said all that, let me say that of all those columns I wrote, after thorough review, I came to think of this as the absolute

Turner, as real as I could make him, with no tinkering, just as it came off the word processor.

$$\approx \quad \approx \quad \approx$$

Getting to the bottom line at the outset, let me say that no one individual has done as much to make Atlanta a city known worldwide as Ted Turner. No one. You can travel the seven seas and not escape his influence in sight or sound.

He is the most amazing man I have ever known. Others may be just as amazing, but I never knew them. He has come farther, or further, from where he started than all the Trumps and Steinbrenners lumped together. He is an odd mixture of genius and enigma.

As of this Monday, he will be the only baseball manager in the world with a record of 0-1 ever inducted into any Hall of Fame, even though it be that of his own domain.

The first time I met Ted Turner, he sat behind a desk in a little brick building on Ashby Street, in the bellybutton district of town, headquarters of Turner Billboard Advertising. It was his inheritance, left by a father who was unhappy with his son, and obviously unhappy with himself, and committed suicide. The elder Turner had sent his son to McCallie Prep, a school of rigorous discipline, in Chattanooga, then to his own college of choice, Brown University.

When he learned that Ted had chosen Classics as a major, the old man bolted into action. In a lengthy letter of severe chastisement, the senior Turner wrote:

"In my opinion, it won't do much to help you learn to get along with the people in this world. I think you are rapidly becoming a jackass, and the sooner you get out of that filthy atmosphere, the better it will suit me. ...You are in the hands of the Philistines, and dammit, I sent you there."

An exemplary student, Ted Turner wasn't. A classmate, Roger Vaughan, writes, "He was too loud, too red in the neck, he talked far too much, drank far too much, and won more dinghy races that I did, none of which endeared him to me."

Further, he wrote, "He could walk into a room of strangers and be introduced as a movie actor, race car driver, brain surgeon, mountain climber, baseball manager, navy commander or will-o'-the-wisp and nobody would have blinked." Understand, this was before he even thought of buying the Atlanta Braves.

There was one professor at Brown with whom Turner had an affinity, John Rowe Workman, who influenced his turn to Classics. He was Turner's favorite, and when later it was brought to Professor Workman's attention that Ted had been kicked out of school, he said, proudly, "I'm sure it was for something colorful."

It was indeed. He burned down his own fraternity's homecoming display and his second, or third exodus became final. But he had his own way of looking at it. "I didn't fail college," he said, "college failed me. I learned mainly about drinking and sex, and I could have gotten that for less than $3,000 a year."

After nearly starving to death trying to make it in Florida, he realized the bum's life wasn't for him, and falling back on one lesson he'd learned at Brown, he decided "the capitalist system is still the best way to get things done. It has raised our standard of living to the highest in the world." He tucked his tail between his legs and

One of Ted Turner's many successful business ventures was founding the Cable News Network (CNN) in 1980. *AJC Staff*

Ted Turner and Larry King share a laugh during an interview in a mock edition of *Larry King Live* before an audience gathered for the National Cable Television Association awards. *Charlotte B. Teagle / AJC Staff*

went home to work for Papa, and later inherited the advertising company, the foundation of his present empire.

With a few distractions, such as his successful venture into the America Cup world, he went to work at it, and proved out his capitalistic premise. He had become a world championship sailor, four-time Yachtsman of the Year, which directed me to his office on Ashby Street that day.

The sporting side of his life took its serious turn in January 1976, when he bought the Atlanta Braves. He had the audacity to think up the title "superstation" for his little UHF bandbox, channel 17, out on Spring Street. He could frequently be caught on camera introducing the late night movie on WTCG, which became the giant WTBS. He was not above pitching in with the working class.

It was his idea to beam the station's signal to the new satellite system, and suddenly WTBS became a "superstation."

The Braves became a cable commodity in 50 states, and other parts of the world, as CNN developed and spread. What Turner knew about baseball could have been stuffed into a thimble, but that wasn't the purpose. Programming was. The Hawks soon followed.

"Ted is a man of conviction, believes in it and works at it," Bob Wussler, his one-time vice president, said. "That mind of his is always at work."

The Goodwill Games came next, a loser on the money line, but a Turner conviction that he carried out at great cost. He tried to engineer the baseball project by proxy, even won a division championship, then fired the manager, Joe Torre. Wussler, responsible for bringing Torre here, said it was all about pitching philosophy, a subject Turner never studied at Brown.

"Ted was a big believer in Johnny Sain [the Braves farm system pitching coach], and Torre only wanted to work with Bob Gibson," Wussler said.

After finishing second in 1983, Turner laid it on the line: It was Sain or hit the road. Torre went.

After more disastrous seasons with disastrous hires, Turner finally realized it was time to turn to the process that had served him well in broadcasting: Hire people of expertise in the field and let them run the show. Hence, Bobby Cox—fired by Turner's own hand, then rehired, remindful of the press conference at the firing of Cox, who had the bravado to show up for his own execution.

"What are you looking for in a manager?" Turner was asked.

"Er, uh, ah," Turner began, then turning toward Cox, said, "somebody like Bobby here. If I wasn't firing him, I'd hire him again."

Good as his word, he did. Then followed the coup of bringing in John Schuerholz to preside over the nuts and bolts of the operation. The real show began. The Braves became "America's Team" in reality, eight division championships, five World Series, one World Series championship, and therefore, the background for the man Brown kicked out of school taking his place in the Braves Hall of Fame. His own TBS now shares ownership with Time-Warner/AOL, a double marriage in this complicated world of capitalistic mergers, but the key that turns the lock is Professor John Workman's own favorite, Ted Turner, who, as Ted's personal Mr. Chips said of him, "He is a man of great, fiery convictions." Was then, still is.

Oh, the manager Turner lost to in his one-game stand in a major league uniform was Chuck Tanner at Pittsburgh. Turner later hired him to manage the Braves, then fired him. Nothing vengeful there. Great men don't deal in vengeance.

—TY COBB—

At Home with the Georgia Peach

T y Cobb had decided it was time to come home to Georgia. He was 71 years old and had lived most of his retired life in California, and frankly, he was running out of friends out there. Not a term he used. Rather, this is how he put it: "I'm tired. I don't believe any player had any tougher time in baseball. I had to fight off Lajoie, Jackson, Collins, Speaker and Ruth. I had to fight off era after era for 24 years. I wanted to get out of circulation, out of the rat race.

"I didn't want to leave California. It's a wonderful state with a beautiful climate. My children have grown up. I have no ties there any more. I still have my place at Lake Tahoe, and I'll probably be back there as much as ever, but I'll be here in the winter."

The Saturday Evening Post had dispatched me to the town of Cornelia, apple orchard country with a population of about 3,500, on the main line of the Southern Railway between Washington and New Orleans, to talk with the "Georgia Peach" on the controversies of his great career, and anything else that might come to mind. And it was an active mind, full of memories, some of contradiction in his own versions. For instance: "I never deliberately spiked a man in my life."

Then later, "I tried to spike only two men, and I'm not ashamed to admit it: Lou Criger and Hub Leonard. They were going for me."

Criger was a veteran catcher by the time Cobb reached the Detroit Tigers in 1905. Leonard was a crafty pitcher who would later write a letter to Judge Kenesaw M. Landis accusing Cobb and Tris Speaker, both members of the Baseball Hall of Fame, of conspiring to rig a game.

But this was homecoming, no time for resurrecting the viciousness of a past long since dead. He had tried to find a place in Royston, his hometown, just a few miles away, but they saw him coming and the prices jumped up.

"I just couldn't find a place that suited me as well as this place here," he said.

He had a plan. He had bought 66 acres on Chenocetah Mountain, with a stunning view of north Georgia, ranging even to the water tower in distant Athens. A motel had failed on the site, and in the abandoned cottages Cobb had shipped and stored some of his furnishings. There he would build his last home.

Eighteen-year-old Ty Cobb cocks the bat in one of his first plate appearances for the Detroit Tigers in 1905. *Photo in the public domain*

After retiring from baseball, the great Ty Cobb takes time to sign autographs for young fans Chris Alford and Tommy Broome. *Bill Young / AJC Staff*

"I'm old and I'm tired. I don't like to say I'm old, but I am. I want to come to roost somewhere, and I'm going to be mighty hard to find on my mountain."

He had rented a colonial mansion in Cornelia until his new residence was completed. His new home would be Bermuda style, built of crabapple stone, situated below a tower that was part of the 75,000 or so acres of the government property that surrounded the location. His privacy was assured. He wouldn't even allow a telephone, he said.

He had come to Cornelia after a meeting of his Cobb Educational Foundation board in Royston, looking for a place to settle near his roots.

First, in Royston with no success, then to Cornelia at the suggestion of an old friend. This was it.

"I've mapped it all out. I just can't carry on. I may not live long enough to carry it out, but I have my plan laid out. I don't fear death, but if a man has lived in the Christian spirit, he has nothing to fear. My father always said, 'Live on the side of God and you can't go wrong.'"

It was a series of interviews that took place over three days. Each morning I knocked on his door about 10 o'clock. Each morning he appeared at the door wrapped in a tired old robe, tied at the midsection with a rope sash. Each morning, the expression was the same, one of puzzlement that was the equivalent of "Do Not Disturb."

Each morning, he would say, "Now, what is it you're here for?" And each morning I would explain. The conversation would be picked up eventually, and he would drift off into a philosophical reverie.

"No new business ventures. I'm in the evening of my life and I'm not thinking of new ventures. I just want to lose myself into life here, with no parades, no fanfare. Just let me move in and belong again."

During our conversations he would excuse himself for a few minutes.

"I have to take my medicine," he'd say. He would leave the room, then reappear with a brightened appearance. About the middle of the third day his "medicine" began to smell more of bourbon than medicine, and he became a more convivial host. Then in the

Ty Cobb (left) presents medallions to trustees Dr. Daniel Elkin (center) and Dr. Harmon Caldwell (right), during a ceremony establishing Cobb's educational foundation. *Frank Tuggle / AJC Staff*

afternoon he invited me to join him in the kitchen, where we shared some of his "medicine."

As we imbibed, we both mellowed in the afterglow. He spoke of Coca-Cola and the value of its stock, and suggested that I should consider investing. At the price of $106 a share at the time, it was considerably above my means, though I later followed his advice. In the mellowing atmosphere, he arose and invited me to join him for a visit to his mountain scene.

We drove out in his Chrysler Imperial and he gave me a tour of the setting. Once he had parked the car, we walked over to a scenic point of the property, shaped like a slice of pie, looking out over the broad valley below. Chenocetah Mountain was about 3,000 feet above sea level, and the view was entrancing.

"See that little hump over there, then the dip and the other hump," he said. "Just over the other side there, I was born."

On the record, the name of the village was Narrows, sometimes called Chitwoods, which has long since vanished from the map. Chitwood was the name of his mother, said to have been a raven-haired beauty. Smoke curled up from the chimney of a little house below, and as he grew more sentimental, he said, "The house where I was born is still there. It still has some of the original paint on it." And as he rambled, absorbed in his muse, he began to speak of the little house below as his birthplace.

"Our family used to drive into Cornelia when we went to town. My grandfather would drive ahead in a surrey and the colored help would follow in a two-mule wagon."

Darkness began to fall and lights twinkled on in windows of the houses below. For one moment, heavily sentimental, he lost himself in a world that would never be.

He took my hand, which made me a bit uncomfortable, and he said, "When I get my house built, I will give you a key and I want you and your family to come and visit any time you'd like to."

≋ ≋ ≋

Sadly, the house on Chenocetah Mountain was never built. He was diagnosed with cancer and returned to his place in Lake Tahoe, where his life turned into a wild series of drunken spasms, complicated by the heavy medication he was using. He eventually returned to Georgia, to die in Emory University Hospital three years later. He was a man at loose ends, trying to re-create himself in the man of Georgia he had once been, but with few friends and a disintegrating family. His two sons had died at an early age, Tyrus Jr., the doctor, of a brain tumor; Herschel, who operated a Coca-Cola franchise, of a heart attack at a convention.

Ty was the victim of his own self-destruction, a man groping for a reunion with the good things of life that he had allowed to slip away.

Epilogue: The Saturday Evening Post had paid me $1,500 for the story, and after hearing Cobb speak with such passion for the works of his educational foundation, I decided to send him a check for $250 for the fund. A few days later I had a four-and-a-half-page letter from him, written in green ink, castigating me for not sending him a more generous donation.

"Now how about you adding $250 and making out a check for $500 to the Educational Foundation and charge it off on your taxes.

"P.S. I haven't been and am not now a well man, as you might be able to judge by this letter, lacking proper form and composition, so please make allowances."

It was our last contact.

—WOODY HAYES—

Warm Memories of a Buckeye Legend

Woody Hayes made the most preposterous exit from football coaching any college coach has ever made. He punched a player from Clemson who had had the audacity to invade Ohio State's bench are after intercepting a pass, and Woody Hayes did not like that. It wasn't anything the player had done. Ohio State was losing the Gator Bowl game, and Woody did not like that, either.

It was sad. It was an unfitting closure for a man born on Valentine's Day, gentle and amiable in his better hours, greatly agitated on his weekend job in the autumn. He was immune to outside elements coaching his team, and I've seen him wearing no more than a short-sleeved golf shirt on a sideline piled deep in

Shown during his second year as head coach of the Ohio State football team, Woody Hayes would lead the Buckeyes for 26 more seasons and five national championships. *NBC Television/Getty Images*

snow, the thermometer at freezing, as Ohio State played Michigan. He didn't know it was cold.

My memory of him appears to have been much warmer. In a more civil atmosphere, he was a lovely man—highly educated, a student of military history, a reader, one who invested little in creature comforts. (The Hayeses lived in a modest bungalow in a modest section of Columbus.) He was the speaker at a breakfast session of the National Sportscasters and Sportswriters Association in Salisbury, North Carolina, one year, and rolling along, first from football to military strategy, when I heard him do something you'd rarely expect of Woody Hayes.

The speech had gone long, and addressing the fact, Woody asked a favor of the room full of journalists and broadcasters, all eager to get to the golf course.

"Gentlemen," he said, "can you spare me ten more minutes?"

They did, and they listened patiently as he finished an analogy of one of Napoleon's campaigns to football.

By the time of this visit, Woody was retired from coaching and had been awarded the luxury of an office on the second floor of the Military Science Building, a quite fitting repository for him. From behind his desk, he could look out across Woody Hayes Drive—no three yards and a cloud of dust, but a boulevard—upon the north end of Ohio Stadium, the stage of some of his finest performances. It was the house that Woody had filled for nearly 30 years.

He sat at a crescent-shaped desk, backed by a bookcase filled with some of his chosen literature: *The Second World War* by Winston Churchill, *Leaders* by Richard Nixon, *History of the U.S. Marine Corps*, *Guns of August*, *Einstein*, not a football title among them.

Curiously, behind him was a color portrait of Pete Rose.

"I think he sent me that," he said.

One of his former centers, Danny Fronk, now an investment banker, had dropped by to invite him to lunch.

"By God, those kids call me all the time," he said, with pride. All his former players were still "kids" to him. "Two of my kids arranged for me to have this office."

All the clamor of football was behind him. He was a man at peace now. He was spreading himself around the country, making speeches, still in demand at alumni gatherings. He would be going to Phoenix to speak to a convention of dentists, then on to San Francisco for a Boys Club of America appearance. That very evening, he would be the speaker at a commencement exercise.

"I do about 25 of those a month," he said, several of a community service variety. The Boy Scouts of America offered a fee of $5,000, which he generously rejected. All he wanted was a $125 pair of hunting boots.

The phone rang. It was Bud Wilkinson, another coach of fame who had taken retirement. His son was coming to Columbus and he asked Woody to make time for a visit with him.

Woody's unceremonious departure had not tarnished his romance with Ohio State. He was still filled with the spirit of the Buckeye. "I see every Ohio State game at home, and some on the road. Occasionally, I get all worked up, but only once in a while. I was at a spring practice game and they left the quarterback, Mike Tomczak, in too long and he broke a leg in two places."

The coach still had some residue of coaching instilled in his being. Not ten men on the street could identify the president of

The Buckeyes carry coach Woody Hayes on their shoulders as they celebrate their victory over No.1-ranked Wisconsin on October 11, 1952. *AP/WWP*

Ohio State, but they could tell you who the coach was for so many glorious years. Woody Hayes still represented the spirit of the Buckeye.

"When autumn comes and the leaves start turning, and the stadium fills, don't you miss it?" I asked.

"I'd coached long enough," he said. "I'm sorry Bear Bryant didn't quit sooner. I think he coached himself to death."

He turned and looked out across Woody Hayes Drive, toward the stadium. "No, I'd coached long enough."

—JACK NICKLAUS—

A Golden Transformation

J ack Nicklaus had come to a becalming time in his career and paused to meditate. It had been a glorious run, and now he luxuriated in the affluence of it all, the offices of Golden Bear Enterprises, in North Palm Beach, Florida, surrounded by mounted victims from fishing expeditions and hunting forays. He was the giant of his times, he ruled the world of golf, and he wasn't through yet.

He would take you back to the beginning, or if not the actual beginning, how one man had given him inspiration.

"When I was growing up, about all I could hear around Scioto Country Club was 'Bob Jones,' 'Bob Jones,' 'Bob Jones.' There were pictures of him on the walls, reminders of him all over the place.

Shown here in 1959, Jack Nicklaus was "that fat kid invading Arnold's domain." *John G. Zimmerman / Time Life Pictures / Getty Images*

He had won the U.S. Open there in 1926. Now I was playing in the U.S. Amateur in Richmond, Virginia, in 1955. Bob Jones was there to speak at the banquet.

"I've never told anybody this before, but he was in a cart on the course while I was playing my last practice round and saw me hit my second shot to the 18th green, a par-5 converted to a par-4 at the James River Country Club. He asked somebody who I was, then invited me over to his cart."

What Nicklaus said he said was, "I've been here quite a while and you're the first person to reach this green in two."

What a reliable source within earshot said he said was, "You play a game with which I'm not familiar."

Nicklaus continues, "He came out to watch me play the next day, and I was matched against Bob Gardner, one of the best amateurs in the country. I proceeded to go bogey-bogey-double bogey while he watched. Then he left and told me later he didn't think he was doing me much good. I did even the match later but lost on the last hole.

"That was my introduction to Bob Jones." (You notice he didn't say "Bobby." Only the great unwashed did that.)

Later, when Nicklaus was agonizing over whether to turn pro, he had a letter from Jones, appealing to him to resist the enticements of professionalism and carry on in the high ideals of amateurism. By the time the letter arrived, Nicklaus had already made his decision, not that even the great Jones could have swayed him.

Nicklaus arrived at his first Masters in 1959, a fat kid with a porcupine haircut, barging in on Arnold Palmer's parade, as some partial patrons saw it. He was only 19, still an amateur and a spring

Jack Nicklaus shows the frustration of a poor putting day when another putt will not drop on No. 5 at Augusta in 1981. *Joe Benton/AJC Staff*

quarter dropout at Ohio State. He'd qualified as a member of the Walker Cup team, and was quartered in the "Crow's Nest," the attic dorm floor of the Augusta National clubhouse, with Tommy Aaron, Deane Beman, Ward Wettlaufer and Phil Rodgers, all amateurs. What Nicklaus liked most was the eating arrangement.

"They charged a dollar for lunch and $2.50 for dinner. I ate two shrimp cocktails and two New York strips every night."

He knocked it in the water on the par-3 12th hole, double-bogeyed and missed the cut. He'd followed Billy Joe Patton closely when he came close to winning in 1954, and Ken Venturi in 1956 when he went out with the Sunday lead and shot 80, not unhappy with either outcome, for he wanted to become the first amateur to win the Masters. That was not to be. He tried twice more as an amateur and came up short.

"The nicest thing happened to me in 1963, my turnaround year. I was still that fat kid invading Arnold's domain, not the most popular player around. Here's this kid with the short haircut and he doesn't look any more like an athlete than Sonny Jurgenson. I remember one year when I hit a ball to the ninth green and it began rolling back off the putting surface. People started cheering. That was a most embarrassing moment.

"But '63 was my turnaround year. Actually, Mike Souchak gave it away in the third round. Weather was terrible. It rained buckets. Mike just gave up. He shot a million. I shot 74 and held the lead through Sunday."

It was in 1969, on the way back from England and the Ryder Cup matches, that the new Nicklaus began to take shape. His wife, Barbara, had seen a reducing diet in a magazine and put Jack on it, remodeled his wardrobe, sent him to a hair stylist instead of a barber, and the next time the public saw Jack Nicklaus, the frog had turned into a prince.

He had won three Masters, but now he looked the part of a champion, svelte and athletic, stylishly clad, blond hair loosely dripping about the nape of his neck, a totally new persona. And with it, endorsements rolled in. The telephone rang about then. It was somebody from Spain wanting to talk to him about designing a golf course. He had business all over the world. Life was good.

Nicklaus had had his lowlights at Augusta National, what were his highlights? Which were the Masters that he treasured most? (Understand, this was before he had risen from the ashes and won his sixth green blazer in 1986 at age 46, with Jack Jr. on the bag. And who would forget the memorable picture of the two Jacks embracing on the 18th green on Sunday after it was done?)

"I'd have to mention two," he said, "1965 and 1975," but it wasn't long before he had separated the two. "The Masters of 1975 was the most fun golf tournament I've ever played in. I never had so much fun playing golf. I loved it. It finished like it was supposed to, the three players having the best year, Tom Weiskopf, Johnny Miller and me, coming down to the wire."

That was the year when Nicklaus put on his most demonstrative reaction to a putt. "Weiskopf and Miller are coming to the 16th tee and everybody's waiting for me to putt on the 16th green. Forty feet or more, uphill. Really, it was the putt that made my whole year. Probably the most exciting putt I ever made, in a major tournament. It was totally unexpected, yet one that I felt I was going to make when I got over the ball.

Today, Jack Nicklaus is occupied with his Golden Bear ventures while managing to find time to play in Legends tournaments and charity outings.
Jonathan Ferrey / Getty Images

"You know there in that great amphitheater around the 15th and 16th holes, it's a great scene. Everybody was saying here come Weiskopf and Miller, and Nicklaus is all washed up. Well, we squelched that another year."

The world around that theater in the grass exploded. Nicklaus jumping and thrusting his putter in the air. Caddie leaping just as high. Spectators leaping skyward and shrilly screeching. It was pandemonium by the pond. Nicklaus completed his round of 68, and that putt delivered the stroke that beat Weiskopf and Miller.

Then there was his lowest of lowlights, in the Masters of 1967. After winning twice in a row, Nicklaus didn't make the cut. "The 79 I shot on Friday was probably the most frustrating round of golf I've ever played. One or two times in my life I've had the putting yips. That was one of them. The other was when I played a fellow from Arkansas in the 1960 Amateur. I three-putted six times on the front nine and he beat me 5 and 3, Charles Lewis from Little Rock." Never was heard from again.

"As a golf course, Augusta National is not that tough. It's one of the great courses of the world because of its beauty, its traditions, what has happened there, and because of Bob Jones. That's what Augusta is. The public has made it so. With the public, it is the greatest golf tournament in the world."

You win it five times, what else is there left for a man to do? Whatever windmills left to tilt? Where's the challenge?

"That's easy," Nicklaus said. "To win it six, seven, eight times."

He would make the sixth, as a grizzled veteran of 46.

— STAN MUSIAL —

A Cardinal for the Ages

I t was spring training time in St. Petersburg. The sun was setting on Stan Musial's long and mellow career, but he wasn't quite ready to submit yet to the fatalistic sentence of retirement. Branch Rickey, known as the Mahatma of the game, had suggested that it was quitting time for "The Man." Here was an 81-year-old man telling a 42-year-old player he should hang it up.

"Mr. Busch has left it up to me," Musial said, referring to Gussie Busch, the beer baron who owned the St. Louis Cardinals at the time.

"I haven't said definitely. A few years ago I went on that tour of Japan after the season and I never did get in good shape after I came home. I hit under .300, and I didn't want to quit on that. Then I hit

.330 last season, and if I hit .330 again, it would be pretty tough to get me out of this uniform."

Musial, his wife and a four-year-old daughter had flown down from St. Louis and taken quarters at the Outrigger Inn, away from the team hotel. ("I use to drive, but I haven't done that in years.") He looked at spring training with uncommon enthusiasm for a man of 42. "Sometimes I don't know why I keep punishing myself like this when I could be playing golf and living the country club life."

Then he slid into the reasons why.

"Spring training for me begins the day after New Year's. That's the last round of celebrating. I go to work, 45 minutes a day, 30 days at St. Louis University, with Doc Eberhardt. He's the head of physical education there. You've got to have somebody who knows what he's doing. You need supervision, particularly at my age.

"The thing about a lot of players as they get older, they get lazier. They won't do any advance training. They check in five pounds heavier, then five pounds more, then five pounds again and it never comes off. I picked up ten pounds when I was in the Navy, up to 190. I never knew I could get that fat before. It scared me and I've been careful since then, usually eat two meals a day and watch my diet.

"No, it's no ordeal for me. I like it, else I wouldn't be here. Spring training has been a part of my life for years. I do it because I like it. Every new manager comes in and says he's going to pace me in spring training. Sit me out of a few exhibition games. Relax me." He laughed.

Johnny Keane wasn't one of those. The Cardinals manager said, "The older he gets, the harder he works. I never touch him. He

Stan Musial played for the Redbirds for 22 years, and by the time he retired, Musial was at or near the top of nearly every all-time batting category list.
National Baseball Hall of Fame Library / MLB Photos / Getty Images

works harder than any kid. He hit .330 last year because he was in great shape."

The Cardinals were one of the first major league clubs to put vitamins in the clubhouse. Musial started taking them in 1942, when he was a raw rookie, and has taken them ever since. "Nothing special, just a multiple vitamin with an extra portion of vitamin C. They don't make me feel any better or any worse, but they surely can't hurt me."

Musial developed a special relationship with Terry Moore, the centerfielder, when he first joined the Cardinals. "I talked to him a lot. He was about ten years older than I was and I knew he knew what he was talking about. He was 35, and that was 'old' to me. You know how you are at that age. You always think you'll always be young."

He has had only one serious injury, enough to put him on the rack. "In 1957, I pulled a shoulder muscle and missed about 20 games, more than I missed in all the rest of my career here."

Now, to economics: Does he regret not playing in New York, under the glare of publicity and the extras that go with it there? "No, I've been happy in St. Louis. It would just have been more taxes and more demands on my time."

Well, just a minute. Not all that happy and rolling in wealth? He did hold out one time, and he tells it best:

"I played for $4,200 in 1942, $6,400 in 1943, then the next year some of us were talking and I said, 'I'm going to make $10,000 this season.'

"They laughed. I didn't realize they weren't making any money either. Sam Breadon [the owner] would tell me I was making more

St. Louis players Stan Musial (left) and Red Schoendienst work out in the club-house. *Francis Miller / Time Life Pictures / Getty Images*

than Ducky Medwick and the Deans, and I didn't know any better. Well, we had the big season in '46, won the pennant and the World Series. I led the league and I was making $15,000 and he added a $5,000 bonus. Next year he offered me a contract for $21,000 and I told him I was going to sign for $35,000 and nothing less.

"I'd read about DiMaggio and Williams and all those guys making that big money, and I thought I was worth $35,000. He raised it $3,000 more, then $3,000 more, and I told him I was sticking to my guns.

"Spring training came and I stayed out a week. One day Eddie Dyer [the manager] called and tried his kind of reasoning, and I told him about all these guys making $75,000 and $80,000, and I thought I ought to get $35,000. He asked if I'd compromise, and so I compromised. He talked to Breadon and got it up to $31,000, so I signed. That was my only holdout.

"Eventually Bob Hannegan raised me to $50,000, Fred Saigh to $75,000 and Mr. Busch $85,000." Meantime, though, back in New York and Boston, DiMaggio and Williams had moved into the $100,000 bracket.

Doc Baumann, the Cardinals trainer, has his own list of reasons for Musial's longevity: (1) He's always conscious of his weight; (2) He rarely gives in to pain; (3) his off-season training program; and (4) his intense desire.

"One day we were running indoors, and I often trained with him. When we finished, he turned and said, 'Man, I love this.'"

The team physician, Dr. Middleman, put his finger on the secret of it all. "It's moderation," he said. "He does everything in

Before Stan Musial retired, John F. Kennedy joked with him, saying "A couple of years ago they told me I was too young to be President and you were too old to be playing baseball. But we fooled them."
Robert W. Kelley / Time Life Pictures / Getty Images

moderation but train and hit. He just quit smoking. Not because anybody told him he should. He just thought he ought to."

And, Dr. Middleman might have added, an exceptionally gentle press. Musial has always been handled with kid gloves by sports writers and broadcasters, and it has worked both ways.

"It's just part of my nature, because I think it's good for baseball," he said, "and besides, it's because I'm such a naturally cooperative fellow." He let out a big belly laugh, poking fun at himself.

Joe Garagiola, his old teammate, now bigtime on television, was waiting outside to do a stand-up interview with him. He had promised to make an appearance at a bowling tournament in Tampa that night. He couldn't bowl because of a sore shoulder, but he'd told him he'd be there, and he was.

Well, as it turned out, that would be Musial's last season. His batting average tapered off to .255. He hit only 12 home runs. He drove in only 58 runs in 124 games, all new lows for him. All that conditioning, all that winter punishment, all those good intentions went unrewarded. Gussie Busch had told him quitting time would be his call. So, at age 43, Stanley Frank Musial was calling himself out. This was the last hurrah for the most popular player who ever wore a St. Louis Cardinals uniform.

— ARNOLD PALMER —

An Interview on Wheels

I nterviewing at the time Arnold Palmer began to take his place in golfing history was an art form. Reporters established their own scene, usually gathering around the player's locker after his round while he changed shoes, fired up a cigarette, maybe ordered a drink, and they asked questions. No structured press conference with a moderator and player on a podium before a roomful of reporters who raise a hand for attention, like school children asking permission to be excused.

Of all the interviews I've had with Palmer—and stretched end to end, they'd run for miles—two stand forth in their significance and the intended result. One was for a chapter in the book I wrote titled *The Masters: Augusta Revisited*, the other, his meeting with the

Arnold Palmer's emphasis on physical conditioning was evidenced in his play; Palmer won 91 tournaments during his career. *Louie Favorite/AJC Staff*

press after his final competitive round at Augusta in 2004. Somewhere in between, there was a session in which he talked of the year he considered the finest of his career, 1960, when he, the Masters and television golf all came of age at one time. The interview was more rewarding than the book, and thus we move on.

There had been an earlier blip on my mental screen before Palmer emerged as a force on the tour. In 1957, Bing Crosby had come to see the Masters for the first time, and at the urging of his friend, Phil Harris, agreed to be a daily guest columnist for my paper, *The Atlanta Journal*.

Bing took it seriously, and after each round we'd meet and discuss what he considered highlights of the day.

Crosby had never seen Palmer play before, but after the third round, in which he shot 69 and moved into contention, Bing said, "I like the temperament of that Palmer kid. I think he has a chance to be a fine player."

"Der Bingle" was right on. Palmer didn't win the championship. Doug Ford did. But winning for Palmer was only a year away.

Interviewing for *The Masters* was not so much the contents as it was the circumstance. It was done on wheels. He was in the twilight of his tour career, having won his last tournament, the Bob Hope Classic, the year before. He was back home at Bay Hill, and no matter how far away Arnie might venture from his club at Orlando, he always had a regular game waiting for him at home. Three retired members, all good players, joined him. They played off Arnie's scratch and naturally got strokes.

So they teed off. I rode with Palmer on his cart. He drove and I listened and recorded. Who won, I'm not sure, but I remember that Palmer led in dining ingenuity. It was the first time I ever saw a person eat a hotdog on half a roll. Try it sometime. It isn't easy.

Arnie has always dwelled on conditioning, and this wasn't an act. He was watching his weight. The hotdog would slide, the ketchup wasn't easy to control, but he never lost a bite.

During this session we got into a discussion of his play at the 12th hole in 1958, fourth round of the Masters, the situation Ken Venturi brought up in a book in 2004, reviving an old controversy. They were playing companions that day, and in his book, Venturi charged that Palmer had "bent the rules." (Some reviewers used the word "cheat." Venturi didn't.)

This is how the scene is replayed in *The Masters* book:

Heavy rains had turned the course into a sponge, and when Palmer's tee shot imbedded about a foot below the bunker, a confusion of rules arose, leading to some theatrics that could only be witnessed from afar by the press and gallery on the other side of the creek. ...Palmer and the official assigned to the hole engaged in a dialogue...but only a pantomime to spectators across the creek. This is what was taking place: Palmer called to the man wearing an armband. "I'm going to clean and drop this ball," he said.

"Oh, no," said the official, (an Englishman named Arthur Lacey). "You can't do that."

Palmer pulled a piece of paper from his pocket and pointed to a line that read: "The imbedded ball rule is in effect."

"Yes, but that's only through the green."

Arnold Palmer waves to the massive crowd on his way down the 11th fairway during round two of the 2002 Masters Tournament. *Curtis Compton/AJC Staff*

Palmer said, "Yes, that's right," and assuming agreement, he started toward his ball again.

"But here at Augusta," the official said, "that means only through the fairway."

"Oh, I beg your pardon, through the green means anything except the putting surface, the teeing ground and the hazards."

At this point the discussion became somewhat heated, resulting in Palmer finally saying, "Well, you don't mind if I just play a provisional ball, do you?"

Even here the official was reluctant to concede, but finally gave in.

The rest is history. Palmer took a double-bogey five, playing the plugged ball, then made par with his provisional, which was finally approved by officials who came down from the clubhouse to make the ruling.

Thus, he won his first Masters by two strokes. Venturi tied for third with Fred Hawkins and the defeat had stuck in his craw all those years.

Palmer would play on through 50 Masters, and so we moved forward to his farewell interview after his last round in 2004, the second of two 84s.

He was a tired and frayed man at age 74, if from nothing more than hoisting his hand hole after hole in acknowledgement as galleries around the greens gave him a standing ovation. It was his second "farewell" at Augusta, the first in 2002, which he said, "was more created by other people than me. I never really felt that was the end. I was more obliging than I was giving up."

Fans gather around the legendary Arnold Palmer as he rides to the 10th hole at the 1993 Pro-Am tournament. His admirers are affectionately known as "Arnie's Army." *David Tulis / AJC Staff*

Chairman Hootie Johnson extended his rule about aging players and Palmer was allowed to break it off after an even half-hundred.

"When were you first aware of 'Arnie's Army'?" he was asked.

"First time I noticed was when guys on the boards were holding up signs. To be honest with you, I didn't know who they were, so I went and found out.

"They said they were in the Army, stationed at Ford Gordon. They had taken leave for the week to work the scoreboard. 'We're rooting for you,' they said."

It was that year of the crisis at No. 12, 1958, he said, but the "Army" craze really didn't reach full muster until 1960, the year of Palmer's bursting forth.

Now we move again to 2004, Palmer meeting the press for his final interview. "I thank you for the support you guys have given me over the years," he said, and his voice broke ever so slightly.

"The press and the media have been my friends. I'm not going to make a big, long speech today.

"I'm through. I've had it. Cooked. Washed up. Finished, whatever you want to call it," he said, a kind of surrender none of us ever expected to hear out of Arnold Palmer.

That was the way it came to an end at the Masters for him, but not a farewell to Augusta National. He is now an official member of the club, and as well as a past champion (four times), he promised that he will be returning until his time runs out.

— PAUL ANDERSON —

World's Strongest Man

When I drove onto North Big A Road, I was sure I was on the street where he lived—the world's strongest man. The operator of the filling station told me I was close, but not too far off, and he directed me to the correct address, 912 Tugalo Street.

"You know, we didn't know anything about that boy until last month," he said. "He had to go to Russia to get famous."

Now they were planning a statue of Paul Anderson in his hometown of Toccoa, Georgia, located in the far northeast corner of the state. Most people around Toccoa had regarded him as a freak, "a damn fool. I don't see any sense in all that lifting," they'd said. Coming home from a tour of Finland, Russia, Egypt and Iran, though, Paul Anderson found a changed attitude.

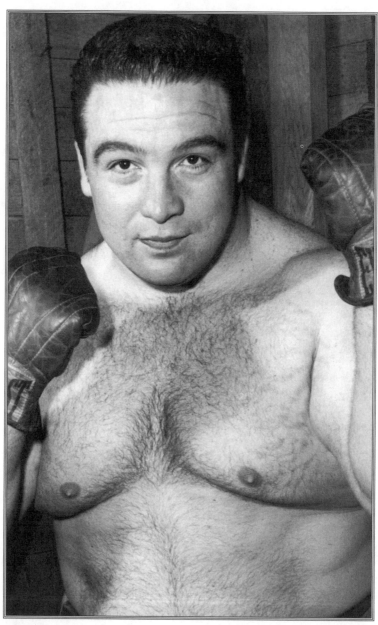

Weight lifter Paul Anderson earned the title of "the strongest man in the world" during a goodwill tour of Russia. *Bill Wilson / AJC Staff*

"The biggest thrill of my life was the greeting I got when I came home," he said.

Television crews, radio broadcasters, newsmen, coaches and townspeople anxious just to get near him, crowded the small living room of the Anderson home. Others cruised by in cars, craning their necks just to get a glimpse of this unusual individual. His importance as a world figure was just beginning to flourish on home soil.

Paul Anderson was only 24 years old, and his celebrity was only in the infantile stage. His serious lifting had begun after he came home from college. He'd played football at Furman University, but formal education was not for him. He'd begun lifting concrete blocks, hunks of steel, then started hoisting a quarter-horse colt from the time the colt weighed 600 pounds until it became a full-grown horse.

"I began lifting to get in shape for football. I'd seen a boy named Bob Sneed working with weights, pretty well built," he said. "I decided if it would do that for him, it would surely be good for me. I made my own weights, poured concrete into wooden box forms and started from there."

One whole room of the Anderson home had been turned over to him to work his weights. His body measurements bore out the productivity of his efforts: 24-inch neck, 22 1/4-inch biceps, 58-inch chest, 46-inch waist, 36-inch thighs, 20-inch calves, all based on the modest foundation of size 10 1/2 shoes.

When he was introduced to a man named Bob Peeples, his career began to take form. "Bob Peeples wasn't a big man, weighed 183 pounds, but he had been lifting 725 pounds dead weight. I did

550 pounds right there in front of him with no warmup. He didn't think I could do it," Paul said.

He was on his way. It was in Moscow, at midnight in the rain in 1955, that he had brought 15,000 Russians to their feet with his show of strength. He was on a goodwill trip sponsored by the U.S. State Department, and at banquet honoring the visiting lifters, he was introduced as "the strongest man in the world."

"I wasn't sure how long that title would last over there. I love milk, I drink it by the quart, but the only milk I could get in Russia was buffalo milk," he said, "so I tried beer. I didn't like it, so I had to get by on soft drinks.

"The Russian lifters were very nice to me. We had to talk through interpreters, but we understood what each other was saying. The Russian papers played it up real big. Pravda had pictures of me. When we got home, I was invited to Washington to meet Vice President Nixon, and everything has been sort of a blur since. Considering that about all I'd known about weightlifting when I started out was that John Davis, from Brooklyn, had held the record for about 15 years, I was ahead of myself."

He quite openly admitted he was not a polished lifter. "I only lift by strength, not by style," he said.

But what is the future in all this, I wanted to know. "Well, if I can win the world title this year, then the Olympic gold in 1956, there's really nothing left," he said. "I'll probably turn pro."

At Davis's Cafe downtown, he introduced me to the best apple pie I have ever eaten. He ate a light lunch. "Ten o'clock at night, that's when I'm really hungry," he said.

Paul Anderson earned an Olympic gold medal in weightlifting and attained celebrity status in the 1950s and early '60s. *AJC Staff*

Paul Anderson used his gains from professional weightlifting and wrestling to fund a home for troubled boys in Vidalia, Georgia, which is still in operation today. *Bill Wilson / AJC Staff*

Naturally, other diners gawked at him, some spoke shyly, and one small boy came to our table and asked if he could feel his muscle. When he put his small hand on Paul's bicep, the boy's eyes widened and he exclaimed, "Jeee-pers!"

Well, it all worked out. He did win the world title. He did win the Olympic gold. Later on, he hoisted with his broad back a platform bearing 6,170 pounds, equaled to the weight of three horses, which broke the world record by 2,170 pounds, and that record still stands in the *Guinness Book of World Records*.

Paul did turn professional eventually, as a wrestler, but it was only to finance a much larger humanitarian plan he had in mind. You may never have seen a professional athlete more uncomfortable than when Paul had to go through the theatrics of rolling around in the ring with such rehearsed creatures as Masked Marvel I or II. Once he had underwritten his financial status, he retired and got on with a public speaking program, sometimes making as many as 500 appearances a year. You might run into him on a flight from here to anywhere, going to or coming from one of those appearances.

The object of his pursuit was a home for underprivileged or wayward boys, which he established in Vidalia, Georgia, the Paul Anderson Youth Home. He and Tom Landry, of the Dallas Cowboys, fused efforts in another such home in Texas. This he made his calling, and the homes still flourish. Paul, however, has moved on, his stressed and wracked body eventually paying the price for all those pounds he had hoisted and the miles he had covered raising funds to keep the path open to young men willing to live by his rules and rehabilitate their lives.

That was Paul Anderson. Safe to say there has never been another man like him, and even in death, his influence on the lives of some young men lives on. And in Toccoa, the granite statue stands in tribute to the "boy who had to go to Russia" to gain honor in his own hometown—the strongest man in the world.

— JOHN WOODEN —

Time-out with a Legendary Coach

This might have been considered an awkward time to be interviewing a coach who had known such an unparalleled degree of success as John Wooden. Just a few days before, his UCLA team had lost its grip on the national basketball championship, a virtual monopoly for ten years. N.C. State had brought down the Bruins in the finals of the NCAA Tournament at Greensboro, North Carolina. But never could you have witnessed a man more gracious and less bitter in defeat.

"We were not unduly dejected," he said. "Disappointed, yes. We lost to a great N.C. State team at Greensboro. We had them on the ropes and lost it. We had been good enough to meet the good teams and win nine out of ten years before. There is a saying I like

Lew Alcindor (later known as Kareem Abdul-Jabbar) towers over coach John Wooden before the 1969 NCAA Finals game against Purdue. UCLA won the championship, their fourth of 10 under Wooden's leadership. *AP/WWP*

for a case like that: 'If we magnified our blessings as much as we magnify our disappointments, what a much more wonderful world it would be.'"

This was John Wooden personified. He arouses in you comparisons to every kind, reliable, stable, benign image you could bring to mind. He likes his pants with unattached belts. He likes prunes and oatmeal. Neatness. Well-trimmed hair. The First Psalm. Young men who say "yes, sir" and "no, sir," and especially "yes, sir."

He is a deacon in the First Christian Church. He lives in an apartment in Santa Monica. He's not much for team meetings. If you can't get it done when you're on the floor, then you can't get it done in a meeting. He's the kind of man you'd have liked for your high school principal. Lew Alcindor, who wouldn't have dared change his name to Kareem Abdul-Jabbar while he played for him, once said he reminded him of the man in the Pepperidge Farm commercials.

Nothing is more miraculous about him than the deftness with which he has managed to achieve with such a variety of personalities and races. Once, when asked if he wasn't proud of all his alumni who had moved on to the professional leagues, he said, "Yes, and I'm also proud of the doctors and lawyers and dentists, and the three who are now pastors."

He can be rather vocal from the sideline, but his most scandalous expression may be something like, "Oh, fudge!" Still, in a book titled *The Walton Gang*, it is written that at one time Wooden was called "the worst bench jockey in sports"—as illogical as depicting Whistler's mother as a retired stripper.

"I never did consider myself volatile. I've never been a show-man like Al McGuire or Everett Case," he said. "I don't yell at officials. I never use profanity. I must admit, though, that as a player [at Indiana] I was considered fiery."

Win or lose, at which he has had limited experience, he encourages balance. "I don't like extreme exuberance after a win, extreme dejection after a loss," he explains.

He has always had strong opinions about the rules of the game, favors installing the shot clock, would put the dunk out to dry, and eliminate offensive rebounding. "In other words," he said, "when a shot is missed, the offensive team may not put it back in the basket."

For the fourth time in six years, John Wooden had come to Atlanta to receive another Naismith "Coach of the Year" award, quite appropriately named for the man who created the game. Bill Walton, who would have received his third "Player of the Year" award apparently felt twice was enough. He had left it to his coach to bring home his prize. Not the coach. If the Atlanta Tipoff Club chose to honor him again, the least he could do was show up to thank the kind people.

There has been speculation that had there not been a World War II, he might still be teaching English at Central High School in South Bend. "I enjoyed teaching," he said. Once he returned from military duty, he found that the school officials had not lived up to their promises to protect the jobs of his teaching associates when they came back to Central High. Principle ruled, and when Indiana State offered him a job, he couldn't get out of South Bend fast enough.

UCLA coach John Wooden proudly wears the net around his neck after the Bruins beat Kentucky for the 1975 NCAA championship. It was the last championship for Wooden, who retired at the end of that season. *AP/WWP*

There is a strong parallel between Wooden and Case. What Case did in bringing a basketball arousal to the South, Wooden did in California. Both were Indiana-bred, grew up in small towns where life revolved around the courthouse. They came from different ages. Wooden played against teams that Case coached, rode the school bus each day the eight miles into Martinsville. But little in their lifestyles were comparable.

Case was no player of any kind. Wooden was All-American at Indiana. Case drank booze and wasn't above raising a little hell. Wooden does neither. He once went to see a movie titled *Straw Dogs* in Chicago and came out of the theater in a quandary.

"I didn't know what it was about, but it turned out to be sex and violence," he said. "I learned later that it got good reviews. I stayed with it, trying to see what they were trying to tell us. I never did figure it out."

The Atlanta club held its big event in a place called Royal Coach Inn, which coincidentally described this man of such distinction that he is known as the "Wizard of Westwood." "The finest coach in the country, any sport," John McKay of football once said of him while he coached across town at Southern Cal.

Pretty heady stuff for this humble gentleman, but one who could handle it. His hat size has never changed. He accepted his fourth award with due graciousness, thanked his benefactors and by morning was on his way west toward working on one more.

"And he shall be like a tree planted by the rivers of water that bringeth forth his fruit in his season," thus reads his favorite Psalm.

— HANK AARON —

Two Decades of Hammerin'

This was more than an interview. It turned into a book titled *Aaron*, published and re-published as Henry Aaron remodeled the home run record of Major League Baseball. It was crisply and cleanly done, beginning with the first he hit off the St. Louis Cardinals' pitcher, Vic Raschi, April 23, 1954. Not in varying clusters but evenly distributed over his 23 seasons. Hard to believe, but he hit three home runs in one game only one time. He swung to hit the ball, not home runs.

Interviews with Henry began in 1956, while he was becoming the second youngest player to lead the National League in hitting. He was a modest, uncomplicated young man, to the point of naive.

Hank Aaron hits his 715th home run on April 8, 1974, against Dodgers pitcher Al Downing, breaking Babe Ruth's record. Aaron eventually set the mark at 755 career home runs. *AJC Staff*

I remember that the name over his locker in the Milwaukee Braves was misspelled—"Arron."

Never bothered him.

Something did bother him. It was a season or so later that he noticed some of the leading players wore double-digit numbers.

Henry went to Joe Taylor, the Braves equipment manager, and said, "I'd like to have one of those double numbers, like 22 or 33 or something."

Taylor accommodated him. From that time forward Henry Aaron was number 44. (And to go a step further, he preferred the sound of "Hank" over "Henry," and to his teammates he became "Hank.")

I arrived in Milwaukee in June assigned to write an article on this blossoming star for *The Saturday Evening Post*. It was a rainy week, games were postponed, and one evening, Aaron and his wife invited me to dinner in their apartment at 2659-A, North 20th Street. It would be the first of numerous interviews with Aaron at spring training, the World Series of 1957 and various occasions later, after the Braves moved to Atlanta.

Some race-conscious worrywarts cried out in fear for the welfare of black ballplayers in the South. Not Aaron. He had gone through that before when he played a season on the Braves farm team at Jacksonville, where it was written "he led the league in everything but hotel accommodations." He had become so relaxed in his early affiliation with the major leagues that he had won the unchallenged title of "sleeping champion of the Braves." He slept his way back and forth across the continent.

Any fears of playing in enlightened Atlanta were brushed off. "It has been great," he said in later years. "There hasn't been one word out of line. It has been wonderful for me."

He had much to live up to. Charlie Grimm, his first manager in Milwaukee, said, "He is the best righthanded hitter I've seen since Rogers Hornsby."

Aaron had no idea who Hornsby was. In fact, baseball history and records were not high on his list of interests.

Later on, as he began to make threatening noises toward the major league home run record, he made it ingenuously clear.

After he hit his 400th home run one night in Philadelphia, he was asked, "Do you think you can break the career record?"

He said, "How much is it?"

"Seven hundred and fourteen."

"Who holds it?" he asked.

"Babe Ruth," he was told.

Given a while to think it over, he elaborated, "I think right now it's within my reach, if I can stay healthy. That's always a thing to consider after you're 33. It has taken me 13 years to hit 442, but I've got a better chance in the Atlanta park."

There wasn't a lot of difference. In County Stadium he hit 40 or more four times. Same thing in Atlanta Stadium, where he played four fewer seasons. Amazing thing about Aaron's home runs was that they were evenly distributed over the years of his career, no stunning breakout, then a leveling off. His home-run frequency was a reflection of his style, nothing flashy, an even pace, no cap flying off his head, which in Willie Mays's case made him appear more dashing.

At the plate, he never had long slumps—except for one that stuck in his mind. "Last season [1968], I had my worst, about two for 24. I'd never had anything like that before. I got out of it in a game against Houston, against a kid pitcher named Sembera. Game tied. He came in relief and I hit the first pitch out of the park.

Hank Aaron stands at the site where his 715th home run went over the fence at Atlanta-Fulton County Stadium. *Rich Addicks/AJC Staff*

"My best advice about how to get out of a batting slump is go up there and put it out of your mind. Swing at anything that's within reason.

Honorary ambassador Hank Aaron addresses the media at a press conference during the 2000 MLB All-Star festivities in Atlanta. During his career, Aaron was named an All-Star a record 24 times. *Rich Addicks/AJC Staff*

"I have no hitting secrets. I have to depend on my wrists and coordination. I hit a ball on the top and it rotates and carries farther. Now, Willie Mays, he swings up on the ball and he gets a lot of distance. Willie McCovey may be the most powerful hitter in the league, but you can pitch to him. Roberto Clemente, he will fool you. He's stronger than he looks and has no weakness. He almost jumps at the ball, his butt flies out, but the fat part of the bat always gets on the ball."

Hornsby's name came up again. Aaron had been shown his record and career batting average. "Whoo-o-o-eee, is that .358 his lifetime average?

"That's some record. It does a lot for me when they classify me with a guy like that."

Aaron was as natural a hitter as ever came down the pike. He was "The Natural" before Robert Redford made Roy Hobbs famous. They say when he first played as a professional, he never had a "favorite" bat. He went to the plate with the first club he pulled out of the rack.

Modest and unaffected as he was, he couldn't help but be quietly proud of being matched up against Mickey Mantle in the 1957 World Series.

"The papers were predicting who the stars would be, and only one picked me."

All the others picked Mantle. Aaron enjoyed the results.

"Well, we'll see who's the better man, me or Mantle," he said.

He hit .393, three home runs and drove in seven runs. Mantle hit only .263 with one home run, and the Braves took the Yankees in seven games.

Toughest pitcher he faced: "For one game, Curt Simmons of the Phillies, odd, in that he was a lefthander. It was that big balloon pitch of his. But over the long haul, Don Drysdale."

Yet over the stretch of his career, Aaron hit more home runs off Drysdale (17) than any other pitcher.

"He threw fear into a righthander's heart," Aaron said. "He always made me wish I was a switch-hitter. Any time I hit him I thought it was pure luck, but they tell me I'm the only player who hit two grand slams off him."

When he finally became the Braves' first $100,000 player, Aaron never let his modesty take over. Matter of fact, at the press conference announcing it—and it was an event gloriously trumpeted by the Braves—he said, "I felt like I was at that level of ability five years ago."

But those were lame-duck years spent in Milwaukee, where the Braves had lost favor, the gate had dropped off sharply, and Warren Spahn, Eddie Mathews, Lew Burdette and a handful of older veterans had to be covered.

Now "Hammerin' Hank" had moved into company with Stan Musial, Ted Williams and Willie Mays. His status as one of the great ones was official.

"I don't want to knock anybody, but look at the daily papers and see you're leading the guys making big money in RBIs, home runs and just about everything, and they're making $100,000. Makes you wonder why you're not. Well, now I am, and it means a lot to me as much in status as money. I've always been too easy to deal with, I guess."

In honor of his contributions to the city of Atlanta, mayor Bill Campbell honors Hank Aaron, surrounded by his family and friends, at the dedication of Hank Aaron Drive. *W.A. Bridges Jr. / AJC Staff*

Now in an age when external enhancements have entered into speculation about burgeoning home-run numbers, never was there any finger-pointing toward Aaron. For that matter, the idea of such a violation never entered even the most suspicious fan's mind. Aaron habitually checked in at 185 pounds each spring, never weighed more than 188.

"I don't work at it," he said. "It just comes natural with me. I can eat anything and never gain weight. I stay active, lean toward seafood, never really work out. I guess I'm just lucky."

And so, one might say in conclusion, were the millions who got to watch Henry Aaron play the game.

—GENE SARAZEN—

Eugenio

For all that he has accomplished in golf—enough for a personal hall of fame—it once rankled Gene Sarazen that he was remembered for only one shot, the double eagle on the 15th hole in 1935 that bolted the Masters Tournament into its majority. "I won tournaments all over the world, the U.S. Open and the British Open, and you'd think this was the only damned shot I ever hit," he said from behind his desk at the Marco Island Country Club in Florida.

But he has softened now, in his 74th year, cozily ensconced on this chunk of land off the southwest corner of the state. He and his wife came upon Marco Island several years ago when Mary was on a search for good seaside shelling, at a time when the only place to stay was the old weather-beaten Marco Island Inn. Now, towers of condominiums and hotels give the island an impressive skyline as you make your approach over the elevated bridge.

The double eagle probably stands as the most famous shot in the history of professional golf. Craig Wood had birdied the 18th hole at Augusta and checked in with what seemed to be a safe lead at 282 for 72 holes. Sarazen was still on the course—four holes to play, three strokes down.

"I was paired with Walter Hagen, and we had only one person following us, Joe Williams, the columnist from New York. We were walking along, reminiscing about old times and Hagen about his women. He was hurrying us up. He had a heavy date that night.

"We heard a lot of noise coming from the clubhouse, and I heard later that Wood had birdied the 18th hole and was being toasted as the winner and the check had already been made out to him. My drive at 15 left me 235 yards over the pond to the green. I had a caddie named 'Stovepipe' because of the tall black hat that he wore. He suggested the 3-wood, but I told him I couldn't get the ball up with a 3-wood, so he handed me the 4-wood.

"From the minute I hit the ball I had the feeling that it was going to be close. The ball didn't carry the green but hit short, then rolled about 15 feet to the cup and in. If I hit the same shot today, it would roll back in the water.

"There were maybe 15 or 20 people around the green, including Bobby Jones, who had walked out to see us finish. When they jumped up and down and started shouting like hell, I knew it was in the hole. But I still had three holes to play and I had to make 3-4-4, and to reach the 18th green, I had to hit driver and 4-wood

Honorary players Byron Nelson (left), Gene Sarazen (center), and Sam Snead prepare to tee off to start the 1998 Masters on April 9, 1998.
Taimy Alvarez / AJC Staff

and get down in two putts from 40 feet to tie. We played off the next day, 36 holes the rule then."

The weather was terrible, a daylong drizzle, and Wood played poorly. Sarazen won by five strokes at even par. "And you know what we got for the playoff?" he said. "Fifty dollars apiece. I paid Stovepipe more than that."

The double eagle was the shot that established the Masters as a major sports event. "Bobby Jones, of course," chairman Clifford Roberts said, "then the double eagle."

Sarazen hadn't played in the first Masters. "I'd signed a contract with Joe Kirkwood for a tour of exhibitions around South

Gene Sarazen presents Mark Calcavecchia with his trophy after Calcavecchia won the Sarazen Subaru World Open on November 9, 1997.
William Berry / AJC Staff

America," Sarazen said. "We flew around South America in a two-engine plane, playing exhibitions for $250, then flying on to the next one. I'd heard of the tournament at Augusta, but I was already committed to Joe, and it was too late to change.

"Besides, I was never an admirer of Dr. Alister MacKenzie's course architecture. There have been several alterations in the course since then, and Augusta National isn't the same at all."

Sarazen had grown up the son of an Italian carpenter near Rye, New York, and caddied at Apawamis Country Club in company with another kid named Ed Sullivan. "One day while we were waiting for a bag, somebody told us that another caddie by the name of Francis Ouimet had beaten Harry Vardon and Ted Ray in a playoff for the U.S. Open," he said. "That ran through my mind and got me interested in doing something other than carrying a bag."

His old-world father was skeptical. "You say they pay you money to play this golf?" he said to Eugenio.

He was still Eugenio until an unusual thing happened while he worked as an assistant pro at a club in Fairfield, Connecticut. "I had a hole-in-one in a competition at the club and it was reported in a small item in the local sports section. When I saw my name, 'Eugenio Saraceni,' it sounded liken a violinist instead of a golfer. That's when I became Eugene Sarazen, though my father wasn't too pleased with the change."

Sarazen was the first winner of the professional Grand Slam, three PGA Championships, two U.S. Opens—youngest winner in 1922 at the age of 20—the British Open in 1932, and he completed the foursome with the historic Masters of 1935. He was voted the "Golfer of the Century" in 1969. He still made the cut at the

Ninety-three-year-old Gene Sarazen pauses to reflect at Chateau Elan during the Sarazen World Open. *W.A. Bridges Jr. / AJC Staff*

Masters at the age of 67. Invited back to Scotland in 1972 for the 50th anniversary of his championship in the British Open, he made his presence felt as more than an antique.

At the age of 71, he aced the famed old Postage Stamp hole, No. 8 at Troon, the first day, then birdied it from a bunker the second day—two rounds, a total of three strokes. At the same time, a much younger Arnold Palmer was taking a total of seven.

He has maintained game condition and still plays recreational golf on the Marco Island course, and on occasion, I have played with him. We came into the last hole one day and I had a 15-foot putt to beat him, or at least tie, and missed. Then he rolled in his putt for a birdie, smiled generously and said, "You were trying to beat me, weren't you?"

As Sarazen's competitive days wore down to a precious few, he became a gentleman farmer, with dirt under his nails and sweat on his brow. He bought a 375-acre farm at Germantown, New York, not far from Hyde Park, where Franklin Delano Roosevelt had grown up. Thereby Sarazen became known as "The Squire."

"We had 375 acres of cattle, orchards and hayfields. We raised 15,000 bushels of McIntosh and Red Delicious apples a year and supplied our cattle with our own hay. Then one day a fellow from Manhattan drove up in a Rolls-Royce and before he drove away, he had made me an offer and bought the place on the spot," Sarazen said.

He had been solicited by the producers of *Shell's Wonderful World of Golf* to travel the globe as host of the televised match-play events between leading professionals. "This was one of the happiest experiences of my life," he said, "doing those telecasts from some of the greatest golf courses in the world. More people saw me in one hour of it than saw me play golf in 45 years."

Later on, there would be other vast variations in the economic side of the game. "I was checking the earnings list of the tour the other day," he said, "and I saw that the player who finished 166th last year made more money than I made in my whole career."

Not that Gene Sarazen ever came up short. At one time, he had a guaranteed contract with a promoter paying him $125,000 a year for two years. He made plus-four trousers his trademark—or "knickers," as some call them—and a clothing line was developed bearing his name. For years he has appeared annually in Japan at a tournament, which he hosted, also bearing his name. And on the social side, he enjoyed the closest relationship with Bobby Jones of any professional. They were both married to girls named Mary the same month of the same year, and were often guests in one another's home.

"After his illness, he always wanted me to drop by his cottage after each round and talk about the Masters," Sarazen said. "One day I didn't come by. When I came by the next day he said, 'You didn't have a good round yesterday. You didn't come by.'

"It grieved me to see him in such a deteriorating state, such a shame to see such a gentleman as Bobby Jones having the curtain of life being drawn over him."

As we parted, he stood under the portico of the club, leaning on a driver almost as tall as he, a figure so small you wondered how he managed to accomplish all that he did. And he waved a farewell, with a smile—a portrait to be engraved on the mind.

Postscript: Sarazen had once said, of his beloved Marco Island: "The only thing wrong with this place is that there is no cemetery on it. I want my bones to be buried here."

As it turned out, there would be a cemetery on it, and when he passed away at the age of 97, he was buried beside his Mary there.

— WARREN SPAHN —

A Bold Prediction

This was the spring of 1957, and the Milwaukee Braves at their training base in Bradenton, Florida. They were still smarting from the loss of the pennant to Brooklyn by one game the previous season. Warren Spahn, though, was over it and full of himself. In fact, he was bubbling with confidence, or maybe he was whetting his taste for vengeance. The dark memory of the flight home from the final defeat in St. Louis had not evaporated. It was still heavy on his mind.

The Braves had held the lead for 125 days into September, when they went into free fall. "It was awfully quiet on that plane home," he said. "We'd lost miserably. All we thought about was get-

Hall of Fame Braves pitcher Warren Spahn's trademark high-kicking wind-up helped him earn four *Sporting News* Pitcher of the Year awards and a Cy Young Award during his career. *AJC Staff*

ting off that plane and heading for a place where nobody could find us.

"I sat there feeling sorry for myself when I looked out the window and saw the crowd below. I didn't know whether they were there to stone us or weep with us. I think it had been planned as a victory celebration, but they went through with it anyway. What hurt the most was that they started cheering us and greeted us so cheerfully that I think that really convinced us that we owed the people of Milwaukee something.

"I think the only people in town who were relieved we didn't win it were the hotel operators. They had committed to some conventions that would have coincided with the World Series."

Now he sat in the coffee shop at the Braves' hotel headquarters, the old Manatee River, primed to make his pronouncement. It made the cover of *The Saturday Evening Post*.

"Warren Spahn Says Milwaukee Will Win the Pennant," the headline screamed in red type. He had a further prediction. "We will win the World Series from the Yankees, four games to two," he said. "This year I think we'll hit them with the element of surprise. Three things go into making a winning ball club, offense, defense and the element of surprise. This year we've got all three.

"We're not a great ball club. We've got our faults, but we only missed by one game last year. Lew Burdette improved, pitched real good ball and he's a tough competitor. Bob Buhl is about to come into his own. Gene Conley is at the turning point of his career. I went through the critical point in my career three years ago. I had trouble with both knees, and you know what they say about pitchers: They're no better than their legs. Last year I reported on two

Fellow Hall of Fame Braves pitcher Phil Niekro (left) leads the applause for Warren Spahn during the 2003 ceremony unveiling Spahn's bronze statue at the ballpark. *Phil Skinner/AJC Staff*

good knees for the first time in five seasons. I've had to make some changes that made me a better pitcher."

And by the time he was through his self-analysis, he could have convinced a jury.

Spahn was 36 years old that April. Two 20-game seasons were behind him and he was about to go on a binge of four more 20-game winners in a row. By the time his career wound down—in the unlikely setting of Mexico City—he would win 363 games, more than any left-handed pitcher in history. And it is necessary to point out here that he pitched in the day of the 154-game schedule. To grasp the improbability of such, you have to go back to the beginning, "I was signed out of high school in Buffalo. I got a $150 signing bonus, one hundred and fifty small ones. They sent me to Hartford, then called me up to the big club. Casey Stengel was the manager, and he was more clown than manager then. I was pitching in a game against Brooklyn, Pee Wee Reese coming up, and Casey signaled for a knockdown pitch.

"The catcher called for a curve, to brush him back, and three times I brushed him back, but never knocked him down. Casey came out raving and took me out of the game, then into the runway, where he chewed me out and said, 'You're on your way back to Hartford,' and the next day I was back in Hartford."

It would be four more years before Warren Spahn threw another pitch in the major leagues—four more years—three of them in the uniform of the U.S. Army. There the rock solid competitor in him was transferred to the battlefield in Europe. He was a sergeant in the Army Corps of Engineers, won a battlefield promotion to

Aging southpaw Warren Spahn (left) talks hitting with Giants star Willie Mays. Spahn finished his major-league career with the San Francisco Giants in 1965. *Sporting News Archives / Icon SMI*

second lieutenant, was injured in the battle for Remagen Bridge, and for that received the Purple Heart.

By 1946 he was back in uniform in Boston and setting out on the strongest run any Braves pitcher has ever had: 18 seasons, 13 times a 20-game winner, and in three World Series, a loss to Cleveland in 1948 while still in Boston, and two more in Milwaukee.

As a prognosticator, Spahn got an A-plus. He won 21 games; Burdette won 17. The Braves won the pennant and beat the Yankees in the World Series, four games to three. They should have won again the next year, but after leading three games to one, they couldn't land the killer punch, and the Yankees had their revenge.

The Braves released him after the season of 1964, and Spahn was an embittered man. He tried again with the Mets, then the Giants, where he won his last three games, moving ahead of the reigning southpaw winner, Kid Nichols, himself a Brave at the turn of the 20th Century. Spahn had pitched two no-hit games after he was 39. He had won 23 games when he was 42. He felt indestructible and resentful that the Braves should turn him out, then the Mets, then the Giants.

What to do? He took flight to Mexico City and had one more fling in the Mexican League, but all it did was delay his ascension to the Hall of Fame at Cooperstown. The Braves, since switched to Atlanta, never forgot, however. You can find a statue of Spahn, frozen in the midst of his high-kicking delivery—"ol' Hooknose," Burdette often called him—in the plaza at Turner Field. It was unveiled in the summer of 2003.

Spahn was able to witness the unveiling, but from a wheelchair. The old knees finally betrayed him for the last time. He went home to Oklahoma and died a few months later.

— MUHAMMAD ALI —

"The Greatest"
Breaks Down Barriers

Picture a leafy college town in Alabama in the early 1970s. The student body is mainly white. So are the athletes. There is, however, a reaching-out, a daring to test the sociological waters at Auburn University. So a group of student activists calling themselves Horizons III had invited Muhammad Ali as one of its speakers near the end of the school year. I had been chosen to introduce him, which meant that I spent most of the day trailing around the campus with him.

In his motel room, as he showered and dressed for another kind of heavyweight appearance, he broke out a set of index cards on which he had written various notes, and handed them to me.

"See what you think," he said.

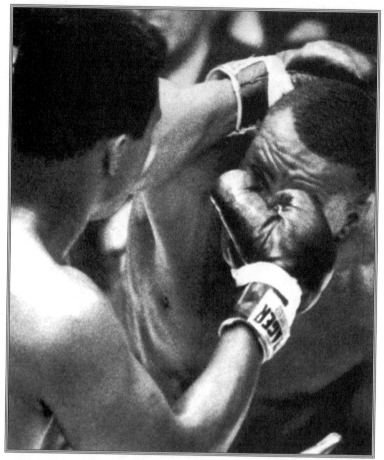

In 1964, heavyweight champion Sonny Liston got a face full of fist from Cassius Clay. Clay beat Liston in six rounds for the title. Soon thereafter, Clay joined the Nation of Islam and changed his name to Muhammad Ali. *AP/WWP*

Notes were made on each card in large, heavy grade school print, and as it would develop later, I recognized nothing in his speech that referred to his scrawled notes.

"It's tough to be the greatest in the world," he said, quite seriously, as we drifted along one of Auburn's tree-shaded streets. "You can't get careless. You have to be on your guard all the time, for somebody is gonna try to knock you down."

He lapsed into an accentuated dialect at the end, rolled his big brown eyes to emphasize his point.

The former heavyweight champion of the world was engaged in the process of explaining why—though there was no question about "The Greatest" in his mind—he was no longer the champion of the world, or how he lost to Ken Norton.

"A nobody," he said. "Nobody ever heard of him. He couldn't fight. Just another bum of the month, I didn't take him seriously. I didn't train like I should. It showed in the way I fought. I didn't believe I could be beat.

"I believe God was punishing me for the way I live. My problem now is making myself work. They need me."

Boxing needs me, he meant—The Big Game.

"They need me. They got nobody that's got charisma, they got no poems, they got nobody picking rounds, they got nobody can shuffle, and they ugly."

He was on a roll, on a large college campus in a small Alabama town, and the incongruity of it all made an incuse impression. It came back and back again, especially after we arrived at the Lambda Chi fraternity house for dinner. Here was this black man, not back in the kitchen sweating over a hot stove and dirty dishes, but the guest of honor at dinner, young, bright-faced white college men of elite status gathering in close to hear him, touch him as apostles gathering at some philosopher's feet.

There had been a press conference in a little theater room at Haley Center, then dinner at Lambda Chi, then off to the coliseum,

After his retirement from boxing, Muhammad Ali was diagnosed with Pugilistic Parkinson's syndrome, but he remains an active ambassador for world peace.
William Berry / AJC Staff

where 5,000 to 6,000 gathered to hear the most unlikely lecturer who ever walked onto a stage in East Alabama.

"Who all has spoke here before?" he asked Jimmy Tisdale, director of Horizon III. Barry Goldwater, Rod Serling, Ted Kennedy and an impressive lineup of spokesmen of letters, brains and politics, he was told. "I'm not just a fighter," he said. "I'm brilliant. I match wits with the brains of America."

There came a break in the swift pace, when he returned to his room at the All-American Motel ("Welcome Muhammad Ali," was spelled out on the sign out front) to refresh his body and dress for the lecture. A kind of sobering mood came over him in the privacy of the room.

"You're seeing a side of me not many sportswriters ever see," he said. "They see me, the fighter. You're seeing me on the college side."

"How far did you go in high school?" I asked.

"I don't know. About the tenth grade, I guess. They gave me my diploma, though, not because I passed my work, but because I won the Olympic heavyweight championship," he said.

"Your real name, Cassius Marcellus Clay, it is melodious. Beautiful. Classic in its own way. Why did you have to change it to become a Muslim?"

"I didn't change it. Muhammad Ali was bestowed on me. It's an honor, like the pope makes a guy a cardinal. I am an officer and that is my title. Muhammad Ali was a warrior 1,400 years ago. He rode at the head of his troops and never lost a battle.

"I don't know much about him, but that's what they tell me," he said.

"What now for you? What goals? What ambitions? What is important to you now?"

"Money," he said. "I own a $250,000 home and two Rolls-Royces and have four children to support. I want to make two million dollars to go in the bank and make interest for me. Once I lived on principle. Now money is my principle."

Twilight had settled over Auburn, named in tribute to "The Loveliest Village of the Plain," Goldsmith's Auburn. Cars wove their way along the streets, already lined on both sides by parked cars. Students scurried about, furtive figures in the gloaming, mostly couples aimed in the direction of the Coliseum, which arose with startling abruptness above the flat campus.

Muhammad Ali was a guest of honor at Morehouse College's Candle in the Dark Gala in 1999. He and several other African-American men were recognized for their worldwide accomplishments. *Cathy Seith/AJC Staff*

"Look at 'em," Ali said, speaking of the thickening crowd as we drove along. "See, at your fraternity I made a hundred friends, like you say. These people, they all coming to hear me, all these cars, they coming to see me. In Alabama, a little ol' black boy like me, and all these people coming out to hear me."

It was not an offensive monologue. It was spoken in the manner of one marveling at a phenomenon, as much as anything else, for indeed it was.

There was a quiet wait in the reception room of the Coliseum, heavily draped in reminders of the glories of football—a stuffed Auburn Tiger, a portrait of Pat Sullivan, who had won the Heisman

Trophy, and of the coach, Ralph Jordan. Peace settled once again over Ali, temporarily.

"After being on the top all the time," he said in a solemn tone, "I'm not getting used to being the underdog. But it's embarrassing to the guys that beat me, when people start talking about rematches and they say Ken Norton, you get a $200,000 guarantee and Ali, you get $250,000. It's still me they need, not them."

The lecture was not Zola. Nor Emerson. Nor Thoreau. It came out in blurts, "The Intoxication of Life," as if the lecturer was searching for it himself. Ali raced to his conclusion, closed out with one quick summation that was over the heads of the 5,000 or 6,000, then opened the floor for audience participation.

Then he became Cassius Marcellus Clay again.

— JOE TORRE —

A Baseball Life

J oe Torre holds one record unmatched in the major leagues, probably in all of baseball. He played for three teams, later managed all three, then was fired by all three. Eventually he will be fired by a fourth, for isn't that the inevitable fate of every manager of the Yankees? Billy Martin holds the record of four, Steinbrenner Division.

Torre was first a victim of the New York Mets, a short cab ride from the borough where he grew up. The Braves came next, to be followed by the St. Louis Cardinals, but it is Atlanta with which he has had an ongoing relationship from the time he was 13 years old, going on 14. He came to visit his brother, Frank, who was playing first base for the Atlanta Crackers, and who would win the Southern Association pennant in 1954. Whitlow Wyatt managed, Dick Donovan, Leo Cristante, Frank DiPrima and Chuck Tanner were stars.

Joe Torre played for the Braves for nine seasons before being traded to St. Louis in 1969. He finished his playing career in New York with the Mets.

Marion Johnson / AJC Staff

"Those are the ones I remember best," Torre said. "I remember the All-Star Game, too. They had to put up ropes to hold back the crowd in the outfield."

Joe suited up and worked out, but no one would have ever suspected that that fat little kid would ever see the inside of a major league uniform, hit the first home run in a National League game in Atlanta Stadium, set a record for home runs by a Braves catcher, that still stands, and win the Most Valuable Player prize, as he did as a Cardinal in 1971.

The fact that he burst into bloom so fast created early problems in his life. The trade to St. Louis cleared his head. He was a carouser in Atlanta, lived in the fast lane, and too often drove in it.

"I can't dodge that," he said. "When you get traded for the first time, it opens your eyes. You take stock of yourself. The Cardinals had just won two pennants, and the year I left, the Braves won a championship. I knew I'd better get my act in order."

It was during a party in one of those beachside villas at Palm Beach, during spring training in 1969, that Paul Richards came down the stairs, announcing with unbridled happiness that Torre had been traded to St. Louis for Orlando Cepeda. Later, though, Torre and Richards would bury the hatchet, so to speak.

"I ran into him at Dodger Stadium one day, when I was managing the Braves, and we shook hands and made up," Torre said.

He never played in a World Series, and "that left a void in my career." Now he has managed and won two, in his hometown, the only homegrown New Yorker who ever managed the Yankees—all the way from Clark Griffith down through Miller Huggins, Casey Stengel and the not so immortal Stump Merrill.

Owner Ted Turner named former Braves player Joe Torre as the team's new manager in 1981. He was fired after three seasons and headed to St. Louis again, this time as manager. *Andy Sharp/AJC Staff*

"You can't imagine how exciting it is. You walk into a restaurant and they give you a standing ovation. That makes New York a small town to me. I remember when I was first with Milwaukee, a reporter asked me what my ambition was, and I said, 'To play in the big leagues.'

"An oldtimer sitting close by said, 'No, you want to *star* in the big leagues.' I never forgot that."

In between managing the Braves and the Cardinals, Torre spent six seasons broadcasting Angels game on television, hand-picked by Gene Autry. During most of this time, Marietta was his home. Like a first date, there's nothing like first memories, the year of '54. They cling like ivy.

"The tallest building in town was the Fulton National Bank. Ponce de Leon Park was a ballplayers' dream. I stayed just up the street at the old Poncey Hotel. Cokes cost a nickel. Earl Mann owned the Crackers, all those things still stick in my mind."

He had returned this time, the American League Manager of the Year, as the main man at the Georgia Tech Baseball Benefit. He spoke to a sold-out house, like a hero returned. "Last night," he said, "I spoke at the Rochester Institute of Technology. Now tonight at Georgia Institute of Technology."

He grinned. "How's that for a guy who took four and a half years to get through high school?"

Celebrate the Variety of Georgia and Other American Sports in These New Releases from Sports Publishing!

Riding with the Blue Moth
by Bill Hancock

- 6 x 9 hardcover
- 252 pages
- photos throughout
- $24.95

Vince Dooley's Tales from the 1980 Georgia Bulldogs
by Vince Dooley with Blake Giles

- 5.5 x 8.25 hardcover
- 192 pages
- photos throughout
- $19.95

Mike Ditka: Reflections on the 1985 Bears
by Mike Ditka with Rick Telander

- 5.5 x 8.25 hardcover
- 200 pages
- photos throughout
- $19.95

Kim King's Tales from the Georgia Tech Sideline
by Kim King with Jack Wilkinson

- 5.5 x 8.25 hardcover
- 200 pages
- photos throughout
- $19.95
- 2004 release

Tales from the Atlanta Falcons Sidelines
by Matt Winkeljohn

- 5.5 x 8.25 hardcover
- 200 pages
- photos throughout
- $19.95

The Holyfield Way: What I Learned from Evander
by Jim Thomas with commentary by Evander Holyfield

- 6 x 9 hardcover
- 256 pages
- eight-page photo insert
- $24.95

Saturdays Between the Hedges
by Jeff Dantzler
Photos by Radi Nabulsi

- 9 x 12 hardcover • 160 pages
- color photos throughout
- $24.95 • 2004 release

Dusty: Reflections of an American Dream
by Dusty Rhodes with Howard Brody

- 6 x 9 hardcover
- 250 pages
- photo insert
- $24.95

Leo Mazzone's Tales from the Braves Mound
by Leo Mazzone and Scott Freeman

- 5.5 x 8.25 hardcover
- 200 pages
- photos throughout
- $19.95
- 2003 release

Atlanta Motor Speedway: A Weekend at the Track
by Kathy Persinger

- 8.5 x 11 hardcover
- 128 pages
- color photos throughout
- $24.95 • 2003 release

All books are available in bookstores everywhere!
Order 24-hours-a-day by calling toll-free **1-877-424-BOOK (2665).**
Also order online at **www.SportsPublishingLLC.com.**